THUNDERBIRD DAWN

THUNDERBIRD DAWN

Sydney Gershowitz

Rutledge Books, Inc. Danbury, CT

Rutledge Books, Inc.
107 Mill Plain Road, Danbury, CT 06811
1-800-278-8533
www.rutledgebooks.com

Manufactured in the United States of America

Cataloging in Publication Data
Gershowitz, Sydney
Thunderbird Dawn

ISBN: 1-58244-118-9

1. Memoirs. 2. World War II -- Infantry. 3. United States Soldier -- European theatre.

Library of Congress Catalog Card Number: 00-111429

My father wrote this book for his grandchildren
and it is to Howie, Brian and Pam,
that it is lovingly dedicated.

— Sandra Gershowitz Kapp

PREFACE

This book is undertaken by me as an autobiography of my life in the army. I'm not an egotist, so if the book reveals a little conceit, it is unintentional.

As the book opens before the eyes of the reader, it will become apparent that it is nothing more than a diary in exaggerated form.

My hope is to lay open the trials and tribulations of the army before the future neophytes of the armed forces in the soldiering branch of this country.

Chapter One

The Dawn Came

It was a cold night in early February 1942, the sixth of the month to be exact. It had been snowing all day and this added to the gloominess of the day.

In a sense, I was forlorn and depressed, for on the morrow I was to be inducted into the United States Armed Forces. To offset this depressed mood, the thrill that new adventure lay before me stiffened my spinal column, and with the aid of a few alcoholic beverages, I soon had forgotten the plight that Adolf Hitler and Company had forced me in that day.

The party that night resembled a New Year's celebration; whiskey seemed to be the guest of honor, and I was relegated to a seat in the balcony. As the early morning hour approached, the guests began their exodus from my domicile. As I felt that last handshake that feeling of loneliness started inroads into my cerebellum, but the sandman beat it to the punch and I was saved from that dreadful delusion for the present.

I was up at seven that morning. The snow had turned to a cold rain, and slush covered the walks and roads. It certainly was a beautiful setting, for one about to enter the army. Ah, but I was still a civilian, and in those last few hours of undisciplined freedom, my mind swarmed with thoughts of better days.

Looking back, I realize how foolish I had been. It was like going to a party expecting to have a miserable time and having the best time of one's life. Getting back to the story, I must admit, I woke up with more gray hair than I had gone to bed with the same morning. I was offered a ride down to the train, but I preferred to walk what seemed to me the "last mile."

As I stepped onto the train, a smile broke upon my face, but it was only trying to hide the tears that were about to break loose like an equatorial downpour.

There were about thirty other fellows in the same boat—or should I say train?—leaving their people and home, and as the old axiom goes, "Misery loves company." I seemed to get back to normal once again. The train hadn't pulled out of the station for more than a minute before liquor was flowing freely, and it seemed as if we were all going to an Elks' Convention, instead of to the army. It still was our prerogative to do as we pleased, and before we detrained, the train we occupied seemed like a second Dunkirk.

About 4:30 that afternoon we arrived at Fort Devens, and it seemed to offer a haven for our recreant spirits; the vicissitude that came over me was unbelievable. In my drunken stupor, I wanted to start on my new career without delay.

We were led like cattle through hip-deep slush to our barracks. My shoes were filled with wet snow, my toes had reached the freezing point, and the rest of my body was numb from the cold and the excitement. As soon as I had removed my shoes and stockings to warm my feet, we were called upon to continue with our processing. Back on my feet went my shoes, sans stockings, for they were so wet it was useless to wear them.

Through the darkness, we were led to a building where we waited for two hours to be sworn in to the army. Once more, like a flock of sheep, we were lead to a minor lake, back to the barracks, and shown how to make beds. By this time my body had become immune to the cold only because it couldn't get any colder. Then once more we were lead back through the darkness and slush to another building where we were given overshoes. That was the army for you, but even in that depressing atmosphere, I was forced to smile at this unsystematic way of doing things. In the future, I found out there were two ways of doing things: the army way and the right way.

That night I hit the hay at about 12 o'clock and was rudely awakened that morning at 3:30 by a corporal, who sounded as if our very lives depended on our getting out of bed. He explained that we had to get ready for breakfast, and when I inquired what time breakfast was to be served, he said 6 o'clock. I was too stunned to say anything, but continued with my dressing.

The cold of that morning was unbelievable, and it certainly whetted my appetite, which up to then had been dulled by the excitement surrounding me at that time.

Into the cold of the morning we tramped, through slush and a frigid drizzle that persisted, down, and on into the mess hall, where I really enjoyed a hot cup of coffee.

Breakfast over, it was back to the barracks and to lounge around reading the Sunday papers. By 8:00 A.M., there wasn't anything to do, passes were verboten, the canteen was closed, and not being a churchgoer, I was really lost for the first time in my life.

Two beds down, I noticed a quiet game of poker. Not having anything better to do, I wandered over to this improvised means of entertainment, where I was soon made a member of the easiest-way-to-lose-money club.

The game continued all day, with one exception. Dinner had to be eaten, and not one of us wanted to pass up that invitation, as Mr. Turkey was the guest that afternoon.

This enticing pastime was brought to a halt around 5 o'clock that evening by a burly sergeant, who gave us such a verbal blasting that I would have been ashamed to utter those same words in an institution for the deaf. The game ended; there was nothing left to do but write a few letters.

Monday morning was the start of a clear day, but the dread of having to wear those wool clothes made me shudder all over, as I'm allergic to wool. Somehow, the day passed and after having received my uniform, I felt my rookie days were over. What a fool I was! It never pays to be a wishful thinker, and how well I know now.

All the fellows received a great kick out of kidding each other about how long it would bebefore we saw action. In that manner the day passed uneventfully and swiftly. On the morrow we were all assembled outside of the barracks, ready to be shipped out for parts unknown.

All the boys from my hometown were told to be ready to leave that morning, with one exception—me. The feeling that overcame me cannot be expressed in words, but was similar to being in hell with only the devil to converse with.

My two good friends Neil Shea and Bill Soltz came over to console me, as did the rest of the boys, but it was to no avail. As I watched them board the train, I felt as if the world had come to an end.

That afternoon I was notified that I was to leave, but for where? That was the question, and at 3:00 P.M., I was loaded onto a Pullman with a few hundred other fellows, who acted as if their heads had been cut clearly from their bodies. As the train pulled away, my heart seemed to grow lighter, for at last I had left what had seemed to me a desolate place to spend a winter.

That wasn't the only cause of my elation, for the preceding evening, after having caused a rumpus in the latrine, the corporal had promised me a nice quiet week of KP. So it was a feeling of relief that overcame my tired body as the train pulled out of this miniature North Pole.

CHAPTER 2

From Winter to Spring

We had just passed Lynchburg, Virginia, when the porter woke me up, not only for the day, but also to the realization that I was in the army. He handedme a broom and ordered me to clean up the car. I refused to carry out this order and I was immediately confronted by a person whose name was Holt who, though a rookie like me, was put in charge of that car. I was later to learn that he was the sort who brought two red apples for the teacher instead of one, thus ensuring his drag. I also refused to abide by his command and strutted off to wash, with Holt bellowing threats of all descriptions in my direction.

Breakfast was served and for the first time I ate out of a mess kit. Incidentally, I had to borrow it, for I had absentmindedly placed mine in my bed in the barracks.

After my repast, I sat down, and was flanked on my right by a big Irishman by the name of Pat Sherlock, whose slight brogue was both interesting and amusing. As the stories emanated from his vocal cords, the miles slipped silently by and before long we were in North Carolina and dinner was upon us once again.

After a hearty meal of one hot dog and a handful of beans, one slice of bread, and some applesauce, I was all set to wrestle a mosquito. As the pangs of hunger still wavered around my stomach, a new stigma came upon me. My vaccination started to bother me. It swelled up like Mussolini's head when he conquered Ethiopia. Added to this discomfort was the annoyance of Holt's perpetual threats, but I just nodded my head, and welcomed Uncle Morpheus who came to visit me with his most beautiful slumber.

I awoke with a start as someone yelled "Spartanburg." I asked why all the commotion. The answer came back that this is where we get off. And get off I did that afternoon, mostly on the wrong foot.

As the train entered the military reservation, a band blared out the familiar strains of the "Star-Spangled Banner." A tingle went through my veins as I thrilled at this song, for it was a new innovation while wearing a uniform.

As we lined up outside the train, I tried to stand at attention the best way I knew. As the major who was to take us over said politely to another officer, "They're a good-looking bunch of soldiers," I knew then he had quite a tendency to exaggerate. To the tune of one of Sousa's marches we marched off to our barracks out of step.

It was a pleasant sight to see green blades of grass, whereas only yesterday 800 miles away there was only snow. This alone kept the loneliness off my mind. After a lumbering 2-mile walk, we reached our destination. A captain hove into sight and started to read off our names and the barracks we were to be assigned to. We were then lined up and led off to the barracks. Everyone immediately fell down on his bed from exhaustion. A cry of attention filled the barracks. In walked a character with a gold bar on his collar. He was followed by two growling bears with sergeant's stripes on their arms. They stopped in front of every bed, throwing a dime on the blanket. As we watched it bounce back to their hands, the idiot with the gold bar told us it better do the same for us the next morning when we made our beds, or he would have no trouble making out his list for extra duty.

The next morning, after making the bed, I found out that even a rubber ball wouldn't have bounced from my bed. Luckily, there wasn't any inspection that morning.

That morning as we were lined up after reveille, the lieutenant inspected each man to see if he had shaved. He had one of the sergeants write down the names of those that hadn't shaved. I wasn't one of them. That afternoon when we had come out for retreat, another inspection for not shaving was carried out by the lieutenant. He stopped in front of me, said I hadn't shaved, had been warned, and told the Sergeant to put me on KP.

I protested that my name hadn't been put on the list in the morning, but to no avail. Now I had a taste of arbitrary rule in the army.

Next was breakfast—that is better left unsaid. Then up to the barracks, where we were issued rifles, and shown how to clean them.

My bed was situated between two enlistees named Pat and Mike, both Irish, with brogues to match their names. This unusual situation lent to easing of the tensions of life in our barracks.

The first weekend came, and I was put on KP, as promised. The first cook was a good old southern boy from the hills of Tennessee, who had just found out that shoes were worn all week long, not just on Sunday. With an IQ equal to our officers, I could see I was in for a real tough time.

I labored all weekend and was exhausted by Monday morning when we fell in for reveille. I started to feel very warm and listless. When the sick call came, I joined the line that had formed, and was trucked off to the hospital to be examined by the medics. I had a touch of flu, which I had probably picked up in the snows of Ft. Devens, and had exacerbated working in the mess hall at Camp Croft. For two weeks, I enjoyed the luxury of resting in bed without being disturbed. The hospital wasn't a bad deal, as I was to find out.

As all good things have to come to an end, I was sent back to my unit to continue the process of becoming a soldier. I had just got back to my barracks when an inspection was called. Stopping in front of my bed, my favorite lieutenant yelled out that my bunk looked terrible, and once more I was assigned to a weekend of KP. But I was rested this time, and fought back with my tongue which netted me another weekend in the kitchen.

A month had passed since I had arrived at Camp Croft. It was almost the middle of March, and spring was most certainly all around us, especially the mud-filled roads that our f15-mile hikes were taken on.

All this time, I had learned nothing of military value and only how to make a bed. Then word came down that we would be firing 50-caliber machine guns the next day. Everyone was then told to go back to the barracks and get ready for a rifle inspection within the hour. As my rifle was in the supply room for repairs, I laid down on my bunk for a little nap, only to be awakened by a loud, "Everybody out!" As I ran to the stairs, the sergeant stopped me and asked where my rifle was. After telling him it was in supply being repaired, he made me go back to the rifle rack and take one out that belonged to someone on detail.

Outside the barracks, the company came to attention as the inspection began, with my favorite lieutenant doing the inspecting. Spotting me as he came down the line, he naturally stopped in front of me and asked for my rifle. After looking down the bore, he declared it rusty, in need of a good cleaning, and a disgrace to the army.

Calling over the sergeant, he told him to make sure my name was on every extra duty roster for the next two weeks. I protested, claiming the rifle didn't belong to me. With that he became more enraged, thinking my protest was a lie. "Put him on KP anyway," he thundered, while demanding to know who the real owner of the rifle was. It turned out to be Mike's. Poor Mike. The lieutenant worked him over verbally, and when he tried to explain, he got entangled in his brogue, and ended up with a week of extra detail. When I tried to explain to Mike that the sergeant had made me take the rifle, he wouldn't listen, saying he considered me the smartest man in the barracks, and that I could have found some excuse for not taking his rifle. That was one incident that made me feel really bad, though it was no fault of mine.

After six weeks with no extra duty, I finally went to town. Spartanburg was a typical southern city, where soldiers were anathema to the local citizens, and were relegated to the bars, where the strongest drink was 3.2 beer.

April was upon us and between close order drill, going out to the rifle and machine gun range, we were slowly turning from raw recruits to men slightly resembling infantry soldiers. With hardly any time to rest a welcome order came down from regiment, stating that anyone who had an IQ over 120 was eligible for officer's school. This report contained the names of those who were eligible, and one of those names was mine. Five out of a roster of around eighty men seemed like a small percentage, and made me realize that the educational system of New London was a damn good one, since I wasn't one of the brighter ones there.

All details for those on that list were canceled and we were sent to the hospital to take physicals. For two weeks I walked to the medical center to be examined and each time the clerk told me my turn was to be the next day. My time was then taken up by going through the books at the library; thus, did I experience my first gold bricking in the army through no fault of mine. Finally the test was over, and back to my regular duties I went. That same day a fifteen mile hike was called for my company; my luck had run out. As I reported to the orderly room the clerk told me my name was on the work detail and to report to the lieutenant from C.D. What good luck—the hike would be missed! After coming back to the barracks, I found out that the hike had been postponed to the following evening, and every one on extra detail would not have to make the march. The next morning when the company fell out, my name again was called out for extra detail.

When I reported to the work detail the same lieutenant was in charge. Upon seeing me, he declared it was unfair to give work details two days in a row; thus, sending me back to my company much to my chagrin. Here he was trying to be a nice guy but at the wrong time.

The company was called out at midnight with full field pack, rifles, full canteens and were warned not to drink a drop of water or the consequences would be most unpleasant. These dire warnings were given out by our captain whose legs were so thin, it seemed he was standing on two tooth picks; I wondered how he would ever make the hike! A break was called after the first five miles. Not feeling tired I lit up a cigarette. Then someone shouted to put out the smokes; it was the captain. He had been following us in a jeep. No wonder he could put on such a show of bravado. What a phony! Something one found to exist quite plentiful in the officer's corps was that.

While we were resting about two thirds of the way through the hike, the captain started to run up and down the column berating the men and claiming that someone had put beer in their canteens and that was one of the reasons they weren't keeping up with the time schedule that had been set by him. He started wailing something about Tony Galento being a four-flusher, and we were no different. I thought that the guy was going nuts; I couldn't figure how Mr. Galento figured into the hike. This guy was certainly a case for a nut farm, and here he was in command of over two hundred men; this was par for the army, as I was to learn.

The march ended in front of the barracks about three in the morning with the lieutenant making us stand at attention while the captain went down the line putting his finger in soldiers' canteens at random. At the ten mile break, I had taken a sip of water. Why I did that I don't know? Maybe because that dunce had said not to. So as he went down the line, I never thought he would put his finger in my canteen. Walking at a fast gait, he walked by me.He stopped two soldiers past me, turned around, and I swear he smiled, as he stopped in front of me. Asking for my canteen, he put his finger in, and as it came out dry he called for the sergeant to take my name for extra detail. Why I took that drink I'll never know because I wasn't thirsty; what a fool to jeopardize my chance for officer's candidate school. It certainly wasn't good thinking on my part.

Coffee and doughnuts were served in the mess hall right after the hike, and we were allowed to sleep until noon that day. That afternoon everyone was called to sign the pay sheet; we were to receive all of $21.00 minus $2.50 for laundry, and they even took out 50 cents for the old soldiers' home; someone must have divided that part up because after we left training camp the old soldiers' home wasn't ever mentioned, let alone any money deducted from anyone's pay. Most soldiers had allotments sent home; thus, leaving the majority just enough for cigarettes. My final sum added up to about $18.00, certainly a handsome amount for a month's work.

May had rolled around, and we were in the last weeks of our basic training. At that time we were in a heavy weapons company; our basic weapon was the 30 caliber machine gun, and everyone was qualified on that weapon. When the platoon went out to the firing range everyone was treated with the utmost courtesy with the cadre aiming and holding the gun for each soldier, so that he would qualify as a machine gunner.

The next morning after reveille, the company was called to attention, and our platoon sergeants were congratulated for qualifying over 90% of the company. Later we found out the reason for their help. They were given two- week furloughs if they qualified a certain percentage of the draftees. Company D up the road had a dismal record on their test, not because they were poor shots, but they deliberately tried to get poor scores, so as not to qualify as machine gunners.This was certainly a smart move on their part.

The bulletin board was always covered with all kinds of notices from taking out GI insurance to getting haircuts. This morning there was a notice asking for volunteers for parachutists for an Air Borne Division being formed at Fort Benning in Georgia. A few of the fellows upon seeing this went right over to the orderly room to sign an application. When they came back they tried to persuade me to join them, but I told them that I was waiting to hear about my application for OCS, not knowing at the time that the captain hadn't recommended me for one of the three positions to which this company was entitled to; maybe I had been lax in my brownnosing, a trait I never could acclimate myself to during my stay in the army.

At the end of the week, the soon-to-be paratroopers left for Fort

Benning, and we later learned that they participated in the invasion of North Africa with most of them killed in their first jump. That was the first lesson I got in not being a volunteer in the army unless one was picked to be one.

That same week the final review of our battalion was to be held, and our unit was to be shipped out to an unknown destination. The cadre kept telling us how tough it would be in our new outfit. How, I thought, could anything be worse than this bunch of idiots. It just wasn't possible. The battalion in its final review really looked good. We certainly were a different group than the draftees that had first been dropped off here in the cold forsaken place that was called Camp Croft.

We were notified that week that most of the men, whether they had learned anything or not, would be in our battalion,and be moved out to regular units, as our 13 weeks of basic training was over.

May was just starting. It was a beautiful time to be in South Carolina—flowers were in full bloom. What a change from the dreary day in February when I had first arrived. Somehow it didn't seem fair to be leaving, while the new troops would be enjoying this environment. The orders for our departure came through and we were marched off to the waiting trains under the eyes of the new draftees who had arrived that day on the same train.

Rumors were flying in all directions as to where our destination would be—a camp in California, maybe Texas, or Alaska. Certainly no one would dare dream that it might be a camp in the northeast.

It was late afternoon when the train pulled out of the station along side of Camp Croft. It was headed in a northerly direction. Immediately cards were brought out and dice were thrown. The usual recreation of the army was in evidence in all cars. I settled down in my seat and started to recollect about my stay in the camp.I thought about how the officers tried to bluff their way through when they couldn't give a knowledgeable answer pertaining to the training that the troops were undergoing.

One such incident occurred during mortar training when the

captain was asked how to figure the trajectory of the mortar shell. He hemmed and hawed, and then went on to ramble about the effectiveness of the weapon. Not once did he give any information concerning this operation of the mortar. Then he got mad when pressed on the subject, whereas he handed over the lecture to one of the non-coms whose knowledge of the subject was most informative.

At that time my thoughts went out to a train trip that about six of us took out to a small town about 50 miles from the camp on a Sunday afternoon. Our main purpose had been to find an uncrowded restaurant for a unhurried dinner, a dinner where standing in line could be forgotten for the day. As we got off the train, the people at the station looked at us with surprise and suspicion.

Surprise for not many soldiers came this far from camp, and with suspicion as to what our motives might be in stopping at their town. I told the fellows to take the glares with a grain of salt, as I came from a Navy town where all service men were tolerated and not accepted as members of the community.

When asked where a good restaurant was, one of the inhabitants politely pointed out the better of the three restaurants in the town, where good sizzling steaks were the rule, not the exception. We enjoyed real southern hospitality for the first time in the ten weeks we had been in the South. After dinner, a slow walk around the town was decided upon to help digest the food that had been consumed with such relish. The antebellum houses were quite abundant and fit right in with the blossoming flowers springing out of the surrounding lawns. It took one back in time to the more flowery days of the South.

Walking back to the station, the greetings from the townspeople were most friendly maybe because we were leaving their town or perhaps because our conduct was docile.We were more like tourists than soldiers. As we got on the train, the people there started waving good-bye. Certainly the army that day had left a good impression; one impression I hoped would not be destroyed by future pleasure seekers from Camp Croft. Suddenly the train started to slow down and one could see the signs of Raleigh, North Carolina. My God, I thought is this as far north as we were going? Then it wouldn't be too bad as I had gone to school there eight years before, and that was where the taste of corn liquor had trickled down my throat.

The train jerked a few times as it wound its way through the stockyards of Raleigh and slowly it resumed speed trying to beat the darkness that was falling on the town. This time I tell asleep not waking until the next morning

Then someone yelled that we were passing through Philadelphia. Impossible, I thought. We had just left Raleigh but there were the signs with people waving and smiling at us as the train passed through their town. One might think these troops had won the war with all the waving and clapping we had encountered from Spartanburg on up to this point, but it probably was more appreciation that we were in the service.

One soldier came running down the aisle shouting that our destination was Fort Devens; it sounded like an impossible rumor, but we were to find out later it was true and it was like having a dream and upon awakening finding that one was still in the same dream. What a wonderful travel experience this was going to be! We were going back to where I had started from in the cold and dismal month of February where I had taken the army IQ test and found out during the test that I was answering the questions with the numbers from the next questions down and had to go all the way back to the beginning to erase the wrong answers and then started all over again. I had almost finished the test in spite of myself when the sergeant in charge said the time was up and to turn in the papers. However, my mark was still good enough to be eligible for officers school so one can see why the intelligence of the 90-day wonders weren't held in great esteem. Looking back on why I wasn't selected to go to officers' school—it was more my fault; didn't I take a sip out of the canteen when the order was not to? I had been conspicuous by my absence when it came time to brownnosing the officers. Whose fault was it that I hadn't learned the accepted way of getting ahead in the army, which was by kissing asses? What a fool to think that intelligence meant anything, so it certainly was my fault that I was heading north as a buck private with a expert machine gunners medal courtesy of the noncoms of company C., who probably were on their furlough as their reward.

We arrived at Ft. Devens early in the afternoon and were met by an imposing array of noncoms and officers with helmets tilted on the side of their heads, and looking as if they had just walked out of a World War I movie. Quickly we were assembled and marched off to our barracks.

As we entered the battalion section, there were platoons of soldiers doing snappy close order drills, and to make it look even more warlike, bayonets were attached to their rifles. From the lethargy of a training camp to what seemed like a commando base right out of a British war movie, it was enough to make one sit up and think.

The men were brought to a stop in front of a number of buildings that weren't dissimilar to the ones that had been left behind at Camp Croft. Upon being dismissed the men were led to the barracks that they had been assigned and told to get ready for an inspection that was to be held in an hour. Upon entering my new domicile, I had expected to enter a residence that would make my former home at Camp Croft look like a hovel. However upon walking up to the stairs to the second floor where I was to be bedded, I was met with a horrendous sight—unmade beds, unswept floors, and two soldiers asleep on two unmade beds.

These two men quickly awoke from all the noise that was made by the entering GIs. They were told that an inspection was imminent, and they had better get out of bed.

They told us not to worry about it and proceeded to go back to sleep when someone called attention, and in walked a major, the highest ranking officer we had ever seen. Our training camp's experience with lieutenants was that our punishment would be severe once with this high-ranking officer once he saw the condition of this barracks.

The major walked down the room and back, nodded his head

and walked out. The two sleeping men had come to attention, and after the inspection proceeded to tell us that they were on KP and didn't have to stand inspection, whereas they went back to bed.

This was a different army from the one that we had just left. Combat-ready troops on the outside, but not chicken-ready troops on the inside.

After the inspection, our attention was called to the bulletin board, where one note told us that there was to be no leaves, and all our mail was to have an A.P.O. 45, whereas one of the men started to cry. This was the first time I had seen a grown man cry, but it wasn't to be the last. He came from New York and he kept saying that he would never see home again. This type of person can be depressing, and what had been a happy bunch of fellows soon became a somber lot.

The depressed mood wasn't to last long as the company was called out to meet our new officers. The captain told us that 2/3 of the company would be eligible for weekend passes; the rest would stay on duty. He informed us that we had joined the 45th Division out of Oklahoma, our regiment was the 179th Infantry and the battalion was the third, and the company was M, a heavy weapons company which consisted of machine guns and mortars.

After this speech the company was dismissed, and everyone started to mingle with the original men of the company.We were trying to find out how long the outfit was going to stay at Devens.

The next morning at reveille the captain of M Company, after greeting us in an almost cordial manner, introduced his executive officer—a rather thin-looking Charles Laughton and another product of Oklahoma, who immediately began berating us because we were draftees, and then as we stood at attention he said, "I'm going to make fighting men out or all you damn yellow Yankees." I couldn't believe what I was hearing, but as none of the other two hundred men protested, why should I? Later, after Salerno, this man turned yellow. Last time I saw him he was riding atop a kitchen truck in a convoy right after Salerno when he should have been with his company, and probably was never court-martialed because he was an Okie.

A new weapon had been introduced to our heavy-weapons company—a 57 antitank gun, so a row of us were taken off the machine guns and transferred to these small artillery pieces.

Our first weekend was upon us and everyone who had come up from Camp Croft was looking for a weekend pass. At retreat that first Friday evening at Ft. Devens everyone waited to hear what the captain had to say about passes for the weekend. Two thirds of the men would receive passes while the other third would stay on duty. All of the new arrivals were elated because most of us would be going home for the weekend, as almost all of the new men lived in New England or New York. It was announced that the duty roster would be posted at the kitchen. Running over to see the roster after retreat, sure enough my name was down for KP for Saturday and Sunday and here I hadn't done anything to receive this honor. Going back to the barracks I felt resigned to my fate; however, when I went upstairs to my bed, one of the Okies came upstairs to announce that he would take over anyone's KP for the weekend for two dollars. We were all stiffled by this low bid. After all, the permanent personnel at Camp Croft had demanded twenty dollars for a weekend of KP. Of course these men were mostly uneducated hillbillies from Tennessee.They had learned well the way of Easterners who they had contact with. If you have a scarce commodity, the price isn't too great and their commodity was to work as substitutes in the kitchen. One must remember that the pay of the private was $21 a month, so a KP weekend could cost a month's pay at Camp Croft. The Okies weren't as mercenary as the crew at Camp Croft, and seemed appreciative of this small sum.

Saturday afternoon came and the captain whose name was Tryon gave orders to give all us newcomers passes. He certainly was a gentleman. What a difference from that captain we had at Croft, who came from Connecticut and was a son of a bitch. Thousands of men came pouring out of Devens on that first Saturday.They all headed for the railroad station, bus stops, or barrooms and all seemed to be of one mind to get away from the army.

At that time there were trains running from Ayer to Worcester, Hartford, and New York and also to Boston, which made it easy for anyone to reach any point in New England or New York within hours.This was certainly a bonanza for the soldiers at Fort Devens. Reaching Boston that first weekend, I grabbed a train for New London. Total cost for a round trip around was $2.50, as servicemen went at a special rate.

All trains between Boston and New York had a bar car, which immediately filled with soldiers. I soon learned to grab a seat fast in this car from which I ordered Schlitz by the bottle at $.25. I drank beer all the way to New London and watched the scenery go by in a manner to which I wasn't accustomed. There was a train that went through New London at 12:00 Sunday night that went straight to Ayer. It was the Boston and Maine out of New York and arrived at Devens around 2:30 in the morning. What a great break!

The five months spent at Devens were most pleasant and seemed to be a compensation for our horrendous experience at Camp Croft. The men from Oklahoma were a decent lot although they weren't as well-educated and seemed to come from a lower economic level. They were more congenial and gentlemanly in their habits than were the men from the East.

After a week in my new company, an order came down for a reorganization of the battalion. Our anti-tank section was to be added to the battalion headquarters company. I moved up the street to a new barracks, where everything seemed to be in confusion. There were men milling around from different sections as they were called. There were a number of sections that made up a battalion headquarters company: communications which consisted of radio operators, wire men who laid wire from the line company (rifle company) to battalion headquarters, an intelligence section which had two men assigned to each rifle company and were supposed to be the contact between the line companies and battalion headquarters, an ammunition and pioneer platoon whose job consisted of being in charge of the ammunition for the battalion, laying barbed wire, setting off explosives, laying mines, and being used as a rifle platoon in an emergency or any dirty job. Then there was the motor pool which was made up of the jeep drivers and mechanics for the battalion.

There was utter chaos in the company. At first, some men including me were thrown into different platoons. I ended up in the ammunition and pioneer platoon (a&p). For the first two weeks no one seemed to know where they belonged. The result was that about half the company ended up at the U.S.O. Club which was about a half mile from the company sector and no one came back until it was time for retreat and supper. A well-deserved vacation these two weeks turned out to be.

Saturday morning everyone would line up and get a weekend pass from the charge of quarters (CHQ), and the exodus would begin—the endless stream of cotton uniforms running for the buses from camp seemed to be a weekend ritual at Ft. Devens. Our first sergeant was a very congenial soldier, most intelligent and probably could have gone to any college if he had been given the opportunity. Willis Frisby was his name and he was the only one in the battalion with a moustache; he bore a close resemblance to Fredrick March in *The Best Days of Our Lives.*

We saw him at reveille and retreat; otherwise, our company was completely devoid of any authority for the first two weeks at Devens. During this time we simulated firing our fifty-seven antitank gun and setting it up at strategic points. This went on until noon when everyone broke for lunch. In the afternoon everyone headed for the U.S.O. Club on the base. It was during one or these forays that a fellow goldbricker by the name of Hardener told me that the first sergeant was looking for me.

All the way back to company headquarters, I kept thinking that the sergeant had caught up with me and I would get every dirty detail in camp. Arriving at company headquarters, I was greeted by Felix Subvervi, the company clerk, who told me the first sergeant would see me now and to go right into the captain's office. All kinds of disastrous thoughts went through my mind. I looked like what a soldier shouldn't look like. I hadn't shaved that morning; my fatigues were rumpled and dirty. This was a disastrous situation.

Sergeant Frisby was seated right next to the captain who was over six feet tall and looked like a Hollywood star. Days of free-wheeling were over and if there was a gas pipe handy I would have taken it. "Private Gershowitz," Frisby shouted out. Shades of Doomsday fluttered through my brain. This was the first time any sergeant had pronounced my name correctly since my entry into Uncle Sam's service. "I've looked at your record and the captain and I have decided to make you a corporal in the ammunition and pioneer platoon. If I had been hit with a baseball bat, I wouldn't have been more stunned.

"Do you think you can handle it?" Frisby asked.

"Yes, sir," was my surprised reply.

"Get shaved, and into some decent-looking dress for tomorrow's reveille with corporal's stripes on your uniform," was Frisby order as he dismissed me.

Arriving at the barracks from company headquarters the platoon sergeant introduced himself. "I'm Sergeant Kans, this is Corporal Rerter, and this is Corporal Rife and you are to room with Rife." Rife was an Indian and the first I had ever known. He was a real nice fellow. He had short-cropped hair, sort of a reddish coppered skin and a slight inferiority complex. We got along well and he helped me get acclimated to my new position.

One must remember that as a noncom, there are certain benefits that go along with this position. First, I had a private room and didn't have to sleep out in the barracks with the rest of the men and my pay went from $21 to $57 a month.

Our usual day consisted of learning the techniques of setting up barbed wire, running the obstacle course, and hiking for a few miles everyday, with a 15-mile hike thrown in about the middle of the week. This was a good deal as no one was knocked out when it came time to take off for the weekend. Fourth of July was spent marching in parades for those men six feet and over; they were designated to march in New York City and up Fifth Avenue. All the rest could volunteer to march in the surrounding towns. I quickly volunteered to buy a ticket for home; I did enough walking in camp all week.

What burned most was the fellows who wanted to go to New York and weren't six feet was the way the army propagandists were trying to impress the country that the army was made up of six feet supermen a la Adolf Hitler. It reminded me of an incident that had happened a few weeks earlier when I was still assigned to the 57 antitank guns. A reporter and photographer from the *Providence Bulletin* came up to write a story and take pictures of our battalion. They told us to look fierce as we posed behind our antitank gun. When the picture appeared in the paper we all looked like a bunch of yardbirds. The picture was taken with fatigue hats on instead of steel helmets and having just finished lunch most everyone looked like they were ready to hit the sack—another bit of army propaganda down the drain.

Everyone was in for a rude awakening after the Memorial Day holiday. The division had been put on top priority. That meant that any supplies that this division was lacking had to be sent to Fort Devens to completely outfit the unit as a combat division before all other units.

That Monday right after reveille we were told to check all our clothes, shoes and other equipment and turn in anything that should be replaced. All that week, there was above usual activity around the supply room with everyone picking up new equipment. As the week went by, there wasn't any new activity that should have come about by our being put on top priority.

Having been made a noncom put a new light on my activities; I had a squad of men that I was responsible for and the platoon sergeant made sure all his noncoms did not stray too far. Thus an advantage turned into a disadvantage.

This new job required me to learn all new techniques of the laying of barbed wire, and using bangalore torpedoes to destroy this same barbed wire. This was a long iron tube filled with explosives and set under barbed wire and other types of enemy fortifications, thus blowing up enemy defensive positions.

New men kept coming into the battalion. As the battalion wasn't up to full strength, my squad was still one man short. It was soon filled by a soldier by the name of Oleo Wrenn, who hailed from Boston. The first thing he wanted to know was if he could have a weekend pass, and he was assured of that. He came on pretty fast. We went into Boston a few times and once to his home, but I wanted to go back home and I had other people that had to be seen, which was my excuse for drifting away because his aggressiveness wasn't my style. It was just as well for he might have been looking for an excuse to dump me, for he and another soldier by the name of Anar were taking the captain of the company into Boston for the weekend.

Glad to be rid of Wrenn socially, kiddingly I asked him if I had been outranked socially. He told me he had brought the captain home, where a good home-cooked meal and the sights of Boston had taken the loneliness of being away from home from the captain's mind. This was to become almost a weekly event while the company was stationed in Devens. Later one of the Okies in the company was in a conversation with a few of us, after he had a run in with Wrenn and had accused him of getting away with murder because the captain was having sexual relations with his sister. I had to come to his defense even though it was without enthusiasm. Wrenn did not have a sister, and I called the accuser a liar and that he was spreading lies because he was mad at the captain and Wrenn.

Here I had been drawn into a controversy defending one person whom I increasingly had disdain for and as for the captain, what he did in Boston was his business.

Why did I let my principles get me into these situations, especially when it concerned people who couldn't care less about me? Luckily the other fellow backed off, or I would have been put into fisticuffs like a stupid jackass; my adversary later was killed at Anzio.

Another weekend was upon us. The trek out of camp had become routine. The 45th sector of the camp became as desolate as a beach where sharks had been sighted. On a Monday following a devastating weekend where everyone was holding their heads in their hands, an order came through that the division was to proceed to Camp Edwards on Cape Cod for amphibious training.

This type of training was supposed to entail the rudiments of infantry soldiers climbing over the sides of ocean-going ships into small launches called landing ship personnel, (LSP). British commandos were supposed to be in charge and give us instruction in karate and the techniques of climbing down the side of a transport with a full-field pack rifle.

For two weeks, the division worked out on the sands of the Cape. Instead of ships to climb over, 50 foot towers made of wood were installed on the beaches and the men climbed up these towers and climbed down with full gear thrown over one shoulder so it would be easy to release if one fell into the water by mistake. It was a good thing I hadn't acquired my acrophobia yet as I scampered up and down the tower helping those who had a fear of heights.

Our two weeks soon passed. We had learned how to climb off a 50-foot tower but not a ship, and had learned karate from the British commandos.

Back to Fort Devens the division went and the hope of most men was for one more weekend pass home. Arriving at Fort Devens the troops were given no letup from their training. Hikes became an everyday occurrence. All training was intensified. The word had come down that a General Patton, whoever he was, was supposed to give the division an inspection this coming Saturday that would have everything to do with the future plans of the division.

The following Saturday, no weekend passes were issued until the inspection was over. Everyone was bitching, but waiting patiently for this General Patton. The division was called out at 1:00 P.M. Saturday and put on display on a circuitous route around the camp. Everyone waited for this so-called inspection impatiently, figuring if it got over early enough there would still be time to get away for the weekend. There we were standing at attention as a car came by with a flag flying that contained two stars. This must be Patton, I thought. The vehicle went by at about 25 miles per hour. What kind of an inspection was this? Oh, to hell with it!

There the division stood at attention as Patton's staff car passed, and then we turned around and marched back to our company grounds. Was this all to the inspection? Would the division have to go on some kind of maneuvers now that we were back on our own grounds? The answer was soon in coming for the captain called our company to attention and told us that the inspection was all over and to continue to do what we usually do on a weekend.

Amid much cussing of Patton for interrupting the weekend, the men ran for the barracks to put away their rifles, steel helmets, and other paraphernalia that an inspection entailed. On the way out of camp, I kept wondering if I should go home or take the train to Providence, Hartford, or stay in Boston. What a good deal to be welcome in any city!

Coming back to camp the following Monday the soldiers of the division found that they had been taken off top priority and for some reason or other hadn't passed the inspection by General Patton, who came to a conclusion that these men weren't ready for combat. His decision saved us from making the invasion of Africa, which probably wasn't too disappointing to the men. He later found out he had made a mistake after the performance of the division in Sicily. It seemed that our division had become a second-rate outfit after having been turned down by General Patton but a nice unruly pattern set in, as we went through our training pattern.

The only one who had experience with explosives was Sergeant Kans, and he handled these explosives as if they were toys. I gathered a good deal of respect for his knowledge. This respect was to cost me his job when it was offered to me two months later. While at Devens, my roommate was Jimmy Rife, who was of Indian extraction. When I came back from a weekend with a bottle of liquor we would always have a drink or two in our room. One morning after an all-night hike, while we were laying on our bunks, I took the bottle out to have a couple of drinks and this was a mistake. Unknowingly to me, Corporal Rife had a low intake for whiskey and he became slightly inebriated. All would have been well if he had relaxed on his bunk, but instead he walked outside where he encountered Sergeant Frisby who apparently had warned him before about drinking and promptly busted him back to buck private.

I felt terrible about this incident when Rife came back and told me he had been deprived of his stripes. If only I had known that he was not supposed to drink.

My conscience bothered me so I decided to go over to company headquarters and ask the first sergeant. Sergeant Frisby was sitting behind his desk alone in the office. "Sergeant," I said, "What did you bust Rife for? It was all my fault; it was my whiskey. I thought we would have a few drinks after the hike as we had the rest of the morning off. We weren't on duty, so why was your reaction so strong?" I pleaded for him to give Rife another chance because if hadn't been for me, he still would have his stripes.

Sergeant Frisby told me he had warned him before and he had no other alternative. I probably was lucky he didn't take my stripes after my strong protest. Maybe Frisby was sorry he had made me a non-com. That was the last whiskey I brought back to my room; all my drinking in the future was done out of camp.

Before everyone left on their weekend passes, there would be a few dice and card games in which I more than held my own. So when some of the men would ask to borrow five or ten dollars to go home with, I always obliged. When a soldier known as Benny Boom-Boom asked to borrow ten dollars, I obliged him.

Monday morning, one of the soldiers came into my room and told me the first sergeant wanted to see me. Arriving at company headquarters, Frisby was sitting at his desk, Subvervi the company clerk was sitting at his desk, and Benny Boom-Boom was standing slightly to the side. Frisby immediately asked if I was a friend of

Benny Boom- Boom; I told him that we weren't socially friendly but I knew him as one of the men in the platoon. Then he asked me if I had loaned him any money on the preceding Saturday. My answer was yes and when he asked me the amount, I told him ten dollars. With this answer, he dismissed Benny Boom-Boom.

Frisby then addressed me in a scornful tone, "You guys stick together." Benny Boom-Boom was Jewish, so I asked him what he meant by that remark and why I was summoned to answer these questions? He told me that two or three of the men had seen Benny Boom-Boom going through the pockets of the clothes that belonged to the men on the first floor of the barracks and that money had been stolen. When Benny had been brought in to answer the charge he apparently used me as his alibi. Apparently he knew he had been spotted, so he set me up by asking for a loan, thereby proving he hadn't stolen any money. Then why would he borrow any money from me?

That son of a bitch had me swear to his honesty and my honor had been stained by a sharp-shooting New Yorker. Worse yet, Frisby was under the impression that one Jew would stick up for another even if that one was a most despicable thief. Frisby kept questioning me, "You sure you gave him the money? He didn't go to you before you came over here?" I denied it all even though the situation was known to me, but this was all the truth. My stripes were at stake but that mattered little; my upbringing didn't allow me to lie, even to get out of a nasty situation. In this case, it seemed to protect the thief. He probably was guilty as hell, but I had loaned him the money. If it cost me my stripes my honor would still be intact. Leaving company headquarters, I got hold of Benny Boom-Boom and asked him why he had done this to me. His answer was that he was innocent. Later he was transferred out of the outfit, but I kept my stripes. Frisby had believed me.

As our training continued, one phase that we hadn't encountered was inflating rubber boats and helping troops to cross rivers under fire. We practiced on a small body of water that ran through Fort Devens. One day the two inflated boats that were assigned to our platoon were filled with most of the men from the platoon. They then were paddled out to midstream where they slowly started to sink. Everyone was jumping around in the boats and having a good time, but unknown to us there were a few soldiers who didn't know how to swim. Sergeant Kans, Corporal Rerter and myself were bumming around onshore, while Corporal Nago was the only one on the boat that was a noncom. We had ropes attached to the boats so as to help pull them to shore faster. When they started to sink we were alerted to the situation and started tugging on the line but the boats were quickly inundated. Thinking nothing of the situation as most of the men started swimming to shore from about 10 yards out, I heard Nago yelling that some of the men couldn't swim and were sinking. He was vainly trying to hold up a soldier named Ranser and as I dove into the water to assist him; he also had a hold of an other by the name of Zairy but his heroic effort was in vain. By time I reached him he was in trouble himself trying to stay afloat; the two men had slipped from his grasp. I told him to get to shore and dove under the water searching but could find no one. Then the men started yelling for me to get out of the water thinking my swimming capabilities were on the average. For 15 minutes, I kept diving and swimming underwater trying to locate the missing men to no avail. Then, exhausted, I got to the riverbank and climbed out. Corporal Nago had done a heroic job, but I must admit I was late in getting to his assistance. Corporal Rerter had stayed onshore and Sergeant Kans just watched.

Two men were missing and as I lay on the grass, it seemed that all the brass in the division arrived on the scene. Grappling hooks were soon put to use along the river bank looking for the missing men. With the colonel, lieutenant colonel, and numerous captains looking on, Rerter suggested to me that we that we both dive in the water to look for the missing bodies. I refused, because going into the cold water to save lives was one thing; going in to show off for the brass was another story, especially since Rerter hadn't gone in when Nago had called for help.

The grappling irons soon located the bodies and they were brought ashore. Everyone was downcast, but it was an unavoidable accident. They were the first deaths in our unit and not even under fire, but they weren't to be the last. What a shame having to die in this way and not even in open combat with the despicable enemy, but these two men had died more bravely than most, knowing that they didn't know how to swim. They still went on this maneuver without complaint; they certainly deserved a medal for courage.

Renter and 1 were called into company headquarters where the captain told us that we were to accompany the bodies to New York City where the two men had lived. Before we got on the train, the captain came down to see us off. He was still shaken up by the experience. He told us to convey his sympathies to the families of the men and to do everything in our power to alleviate their suffering because of this accident. I had never seen him so concerned about a situation before and was really overtaken by his sympathetic gesture.

I was picked to go along with one of the bodies because Zairy was Jewish and Rerter was picked because Ranser was Protestant.

As the train pulled away, I winced thinking of meeting with the families of the men. The train pulled into the station in New York about one P.M. and as we left the coach to go back to the baggage car where the bodies were, the crowds were immense. I had never been in Grand Central Station during wartime and never realized how many people could crowd onto a station platform; it looked like a scene at a World Series at Yankee Stadium. However when we reached the baggage car, the caskets were already being wheeled off the train. The crowd parted and one could feel the trauma in the people as they gazed down at the flag-draped caskets. Most probably thought they were KIA (killed in action). As the caskets were pushed along, the crowds parted in silence and we moved to the baggage room of the station, where a graves' registration officer met us with two funeral directors and took the caskets away.

Rerter and I were given a hotel to go to on Fifth Avenue and orders to attend a funeral home the next morning.

A night in New York City was the dream of every GI, but who knew where to go? As honor guards for the bodies, we were given sidearms and there we were walking around Broadway with a 45-caliber pistol attached to our hip. Walking along 56th Street, toward 9th Avenue, we encountered a bootblack who offered to shine our shoes. Taking up his offer we had our shoes shined, whereas he demanded a dollar apiece for the shine, an outrageous price and a stupid demand, especially from two soldiers carrying 45's.

Rerter immediately drew out his 45 and threatened to shoot the man who was Black. One must remember that he came from Oklahoma where Blacks were held in low esteem. "N....," he yelled, as he threw a half dollar at him, "Take this or I'll blow your head off." He pointed the pistol at the man. I don't know who was more scared—the bootblack or me. Grabbing Rerter by the arm and trying to pull him away before he pulled the trigger was an ordeal I wouldn't want to encounter again. As we walked up the street, Rerter was still enraged and doing the best to quiet him, I pulled him into a bar, where we sat down at a table. Over a couple of beers he raved on about what he should have done to that Black man. What a jam we would have been in if he had pulled that trigger!

The first shadows of the evening were falling as we went back to the hotel and it was a good thing, as we seemed to become more conspicuous as we walked along with the pistols hanging from our gun belts. After all the only soldiers that wore side arms were the MPs. Arriving at the hotel, I went over to the desk clerk and tried to get a safety deposit box to check our guns. The clerk was mystified as to why we would want to get rid of our arms and called over the manager to whom I explained that we didn't want to go around New York armed that evening as we wished to spend a normal night in the city. He seemed to think we were on a special mission of intrigue, but he accepted our weapons and put them in a large deposit box.

Leaving the hotel, we strolled up Fifth Avenue toward Central Park and as we reached the first benches, two young ladies were sitting there and enjoying the night air. We struck up a conversation. They soon informed us that they were nurses and worked at a hospital in Brooklyn. As we hadn't had supper yet, we invited them to have supper with us and to let us know where there was a good restaurant to eat as they were more knowledgeable about the eating places in New York.

The one who seemed to be more interested in me and seemed to have picked me as her partner stood up and I almost sat down. She was over six feet tall and the thought of going into a public place or even walking through the streets with her made me wish I had kept walking by these girls, but hell I thought, if she didn't mind going with me, why should I mind?

Hailing a cab we drove down to around 45th Street and Broadway where we got out of the cab and the girls led us up some stairs to what turned out to be a quite famous restaurant of Chinese origin. There was a good orchestra playing as we entered and having lost the fright of her size strolled right over to a table before we became too conspicuous and where a double shot of 100-proof Old-Overholt soon brought me to an equal footing.

After dinner and a few more shots of whiskey I was soon gliding over the dance floor. It was like driving blindfolded. When the bill came, I felt a hand under the table. It was that of my companion. In her hand were two twenties, which she tried to pass to me but I refused until she kept insisting that I take them to pay for the dinner. I thought to myself, had I joined the army to become a gigolo? No, I told myself, the girl knew our pay was limited and she was taking the army out as her part of the war effort.

The next morning, it was tough to wake up. My head wasn't back to normal and I had to meet the family of the boy who had drowned. On the subway ride to the Bronx where the funeral home was located I kept wondering how many more men that I knew would have their lives ended by this conflict. What a shame for this young man! Upon entering the funeral home, I was handed a telegram from the secretary of the army in which he sent his condolences to the family.

The funeral director asked me to read it and offer a few words of my own about the deceased. That was my first attempt at public speaking and something I wouldn't have wished upon my worst enemy.

After the funeral I went back to the hotel where I met Corporal Rerter. His job was even more distasteful than mine. The only relative of this soldier was the man's mother and his eyes were still red from the tears. I wanted to stay in New York for another night but he insisted on going back to camp. So back we went, but I got off in New London and let him continue back to Fort Devens.

Two days after I got back, a directive came down that anyone whose IQ made him eligible for officer's school could apply for the Air Corps Officers' School. I put in my application and waited to hear if I would be accepted. A week later the division was ordered to move out to Pine Camp which was located in Watertown, New York, not far from the Canadian border. What the hell were we going to do up there? I guess everyone thought we were going to go to the Aleutian Islands and the army was going to give us some training in real winter weather.

It was late October as we moved out of Devens. With that move, an order came down that no more men would be transferred out; there went my hopes to go to the air corps.

Arriving at Pine Camp it was a real winter scene; a foot of snow had already fallen. It seemed we had reached the North Pole with the snow and cold temperature. We were issued parkas to protect us from the cold and I felt as if I were an Eskimo. Luckily I had bought two officers' shirts that weren't wool as we were back to wearing khakis instead of suntans.

Of course, at this time I didn't know that one could be discharged for being allergic to wool. As the weeks went by, the snow kept getting higher and the camp seemed to be more isolated than ever. An occasional foray into Watertown wasn't much better than being in camp.

There was a train that ran from Watertown to Utica, Albany, Springfield, and Boston which got a fair share of passengers every weekend. Syracuse was about 80 miles south and excursions by bus were utilized to the fullest by the men at the camp almost every weekend. One must remember that the division originated in Oklahoma, a dry state. When it first came north to Boston, this was the first legal liquor the men from Oklahoma had ever seen and the effect was as if a herd of horses had just come from a desert.

One episode remains in my mind while walking along the streets of Watertown. I passed by a Sergeant Hightower, who was in the communication platoon. He was out walking with his wife who was pregnant and looked to be about in her seventh month. He introduced her. She seemed to be a very pleasant woman. This episode stood out in my mind because he was killed at Anzio and I always wondered if he had ever seen his child. I always felt sorry for her plight especially when she received that deplorable telegram.

Christmas was coming in a few days and almost everyone had a three- or five-day pass! Some men had already left, so when I happened to bump into Sergeant Frisby in downtown Watertown, he mentioned to me that we were the few who would be spending the holidays at Pine Camp, and asked why I hadn't applied for a three-day pass to go home. I told him it wasn't my holiday and felt guilty about asking for a pass that might deprive someone of the Christian faith from going home. Since many of the men were from Oklahoma and most would be staying in camp, if I wanted a pass he would gladly give me one. So off I went back to New London for the next-to-last trip I would get home.

The train on the way back was late in getting to camp. Everyone was supposed to report for duty by 7:00 A.M. but the train didn't arrive until noon. Most of the officers had been to Boston to see their paramours or other sundry reasons and were indistinguishable from the Morpheus-laden enlisted men on the train who smelled like a liquor warehouse where a bolt of lightning had struck all the barrels of whiskey open. With almost everyone as sober as participants at a St. Patrick's Day party where the drinks were free, how could any of the soldiers be held accountable for being late when half the officers of the division were involved? This wasn't the first time this had occurred but everyone was protected, especially the non-officer class.

What training that was done was confined to the barracks or whatever inside space that could be found, as the weather wasn't conducive to outside maneuvers. I received most of my training in explosives at Pine Camp from real professionals, though the near-zero-degree weather made it most hazardous to handle dynamite. We were warned by our instructors that this type of weather made these explosives most sensitive. Luckily no accidents occurred during this training.

A few of the men were picked for special training in Florida and one of the men was Corporal Rerter; I wondered why they were being sent to Florida while we all took training in this North Pole-type of atmosphere. During this period, the question of seniority came up for the first time for me since I had been in the army. Sergeant Kans who was the platoon sergeant had a run in with a Lieutenant Shanks, who was the executive officer of the company. I was called over to the orderly room and told to report to Lieutenant Shanks. Upon reporting to the lieutenant, he told me he was putting me in charge of the platoon, as he had no confidence in Sergeant Kans's ability to follow orders. Since I was an idiot, I protested to him that Sergeant Kans was an expert in explosives and the platoon would be losing a valuable leader. (Sergeant Kans never set off one explosive charge in combat. He was captured the fourth day in Sicily.)

There I was protecting a man who, without my knowledge, was trying to get me busted. All the while he was claiming I was after his job when it really was Corporals Rerter and Nago who were hot after his job, though I was senior to both of these men. Lieutenant Shanks was stunned that I came to Sergeant Kans' defense and he angrily dismissed me. From that time on, whenever he had to pick a noncom to oversee a detail, he acted as it I wasn't in the company and Sergeant Kans kept going around saying that the New Yorkers were trying to get his job. I told him he couldn't mean me since I came from New

London and Corporal Rogo came from New York. I had saved his job and all I got for it was his damn innuendoes.

The first week in January had passed, and as the men half slumbered in this frozen wasteland, the division was alerted to a possible move. All the heavy clothing was to be turned in and packing of all regular equipment was to begin as soon as possible. Then on January 10, we were told the division would move out in the next few days, but to where was a deep secret. The rumors started to fly; it could be to the Pacific or Europe or maybe to the Panama Canal Zone.

On January 12, we were marched to the trains that were waiting at a rail spur in camp. I relaxed on a seat in the train and watched the high walls of snow pass by, as the train slowly moved out of the camp. Thoughts of a year earlier came to my mind when I had gotten on a train headed for Camp Croft in South Carolina. Then I was a raw recruit. Now a year later, I was a fairly well-trained soldier.

What a difference a year made: no ambitious recruit telling me to clean up the car, smoking whenever one pleased, food served regularly and hot, and for entertainment, all the poker games one wished to partake in, even the bigger ones which not only consisted of the enlisted men, but a mixture of noncoms and officers which usually were for higher stakes. So if one had the money, any one was eligible to participate. Because I was one of the more affluent members of the company, due to my not having any allotment money going home and my luck at the games of chance, I naturally ended up at the game with the highest stakes which was made up of officers and noncoms from the battalion. During one game I was sitting next to Sergeant Maris, who was the mess sergeant of my company and who always seemed to have good luck at cards. About 2:00 in the morning, after about four hours of playing, my luck had filtered down to my last $30, so with two pairs and the last card coming up, I bet $10. Maris raised me $20 and at the same time, lifted his two bottom cards which were aces and with one showing he had three aces. I knew I was beaten, but just then a lieutenant tapped him on the shoulder and told him to throw his cards in and leave. Unknown to me he had slipped an ace into his hand and as these men had played with him before, they were watching him closely. He just got up and walked away; whereupon, I gathered in the pot as I had the next best hand. That was the last time I played cards with Maris but our friendship didn't end there as he was a most likable fellow and being on friendly terms with the mess sergeant didn't hurt one's diet. He was, in the lexicon of the time, a fast operator but not illegitimate in his operations. His only flaw was his joy of being able to pull an ace out of his sleeve unbeknownst to his fellow card players. Poor fellow—he was later killed in Italy. This taught me a lesson, and that was not to try to get some thing that wasn't mine.

About 10:00 in the morning the troop train started to slow down as it approached a railroad station whose signs said Philadelphia. As the train came to a jerky halt, an order ran through the cars for every one to detrain.

The cars started to unload and everyone wandered around in the brisk air of Philadelphia. What a change from the Alaskan weather of Pine Camp! A sharp order came down to the troops telling them to take their morning calisthenics. With civilian travelers in the station looking on, the troops went through a half hour of exercises. The civilian onlookers must have thought what were such well-trained troops still doing in the states, when these soldiers should be out killing the sons of Nippon or the barbarian hordes that call themselves Germans.

The train whistle blew and the men were back on the train before the civilians finished giving them a patriotic hand-clapping. Another phase of my army life was ending and as the train slowly pulled out of the station, some of the people left behind seemed to wish that they were accompanying us on our adventure.

It was late afternoon as we pulled into our last training station—Camp Pickett. It was located about 50 miles east of Lynchburg, Virginia, and about 60 miles south of Richmond. Even though it was January, the difference in weather at Pickett from Pine Camp was such that it was more pleasant to be outside at Pickett than inside at

Pine Camp. The barracks seemed to be the same at all camps but my noncom stripes entitled me to have a sort of semiprivate room, this time with the two other corporals, Rerter and Nago. Rerter hadn't returned from his special training as yet, so Nago and I enjoyed this large room by ourselves.

Training started as soon as we unpacked; fifteen-mile hikes became as common place as breakfast. When the first weekend came, everyone made a private reconnoiter of the camp. It was a large training area; it had everything from medic training to the infantry. Luckily the barracks weren't situated too far from the PX, where I usually sent someone over to pick up the Richmond *Times* every morning before our training started. The paper came in handy during our lunch break in the field. I could read the paper while dining, usually using a large boulder to sit on with the paper spread out in front of me and slowly digesting what the mess sergeant had concocted for lunch—much to the annoyance of the platoon sergeant. I was not ready to join the platoon until I had done most of my reading. Our platoon had been devoid of a platoon lieutenant for about two months. Sergeant Kans was in command and there was no love lost between us, especially since he knew I had been offered his job. The little town outside the camp was just that—a honky-tonk, with gin mills, cheap souvenir stores, and the usual camp followers. For the few married men in the company it became an ordeal to find a place to live for their wives. Of course their plight didn't much bother me. After all, who told them to get married, especially with a war about to start or already started. Funny with all the girls I had gone out with marriage had never entered my mind. So why the hell had these men gotten married? Of course I was being callous using myself as a barometer, but why should I worry about their plight? Yet I did have a certain sympathy for their hardship in obtaining lodging outside of camp. Gouging by the landlords was as common as the khaki uniforms that filled the camp. One such soldier was George who came from Massachusetts, with whom I had become very friendly. At the time he had just gotten married and lived off camp.

Every morning he would arrive at the barracks just before reveille. Never too heavy, he would seem to be getting thinner every day. So I dubbed him the "Window Shade Kid," and every morning when he would arrive at the barracks, I would pull up an imaginary window shade and make believe it was pulling me up, trying to give a good imitation of him. He took it in a good-natured manner, and it always brought a good laugh in the barracks. When I think about it today, maybe it was a little too harsh.

Trying to get away from the barracks on weekends wasn't too hard but where to go? I soon discovered that a train ran to Lynchburg from camp and came by this way a few times a day. So with another soldier by the name of Sudy, my weekends usually ended up in that city, where it was a rarity to see a soldier and these people were most hospitable.

Liquor was rationed in Virginia and one needed a ration coupon to obtain a bottle, but these were issued at camp. Even when I forgot to get one, people in Lynchburg would gladly give one to you. They were a very friendly lot, I must say. The hotel where I stayed was most inviting. Privacy had become a luxury in the army and just to be able to sleep late on a Sunday morning was worth the trip, not counting the sundry things while there.

Soon our training intensified. Whereas weekends had been open, overnight hikes and field maneuvers soon eliminated them. The weeks ran into months and it was late April when we got a platoon lieutenant by the name of Russo. He had come from a military school. When he took over the platoon he thought he was still at that school. It was bad enough to be training all day but he gave an order that he wanted his noncoms to go through a special training in close order drill for an hour after supper. Sergeant Kans refused to go and that put him on Lieutenant Russo's shit list, but what surprised him most was that of all the noncoms, I was the most proficient at close order drill.

An order came down that the division was to go on amphibious maneuvers the following week, and we were going to get a chance to put to use all that we had learned at Camp Edwards in Massachusetts. With the weekend coming up Sergeant Maris, the mess sergeant, operator that he was, had somehow gotten hold of two cars and was carrying on a transportation system of his own, using the cars to transport soldiers to Washington where one could catch a train for home. The captain, Wrenn, and four other fellows filled up one car. I went with Maris, his wife and four other fellows in the other car, figuring to spend the weekend in Washington, since we wouldn't be arriving until late Saturday afternoon at the train station. On the way sitting in the front seat with Maris and his wife, a car passed us and cut sharply in front of our car. Marisa's wife said "Where the fuck is he going?" Never having heard a woman use this epithet, my face reddened. Then Maris yelled, "You fucking bastard," at the other car, whereas I was left most embarrassed, though no one else seemed the least annoyed. Funny, I used that adjective in camp as part of my regular vocabulary at all times but never in front of a woman, even one of the lowest caliber. Arriving at the station I found that the train that the other fellows were taking to Boston was going by way of Hartford and the next train to New London didn't leave until ten P.M., so I told Maris that I was going to spend the weekend in Washington. He gave me the keys to one of the cars and told me to park it at the station parking lot as that was where everyone was to meet on the way home.

Washington had several U.S.O. clubs for soldiers, but I drove around looking for a hotel. As they were all full, I started wondering that maybe I should catch the 10 o'clock train to Boston, which would land me in New London about 6 A.M., but I would have to grab a 4 o'clock train the same day to get back to Washington. This probably would be my last trip home, so I bought a ticket for home.

Arriving in New London about six A.M. after having slept all the way home, my family was surprised and glad to see me. In the short period of time we had together, gifts of liquor soon filled up a small suitcase that my brother found somewhere and the only friend that I had left in New London, Morris Rutberg, drove me to the station.

He put a bottle of Canadian Club in my hands as I boarded the train.

Getting adjusted to a seat on the train was easy as I had been drinking all day and as the train headed for New York, the people were most friendly and everyone seemed to have a bottle handy, especially for a soldier who was making his last trip home.

Arriving at the Washington station half under the weather, I noticed a group of soldiers yelling "here he is," and the next thing I knew I was lifted bodily into the air as I alighted from the train. I had the key to the second car and the passengers that had come up with me had been waiting about four hours for me to arrive. They were sure glad to see me, but they sure acted physical. The way they held me aloft it was a good thing I hadn't lost the key to the car. However, when we got in the car and started out, I opened my suitcase and before long everyone was feeling as well as me, except for the driver who wisely turned down the bottle that was offered. Soon everyone's private life became an open book as the whiskey flowed through their veins.

Out of the seven of us packed into the car, three were killed in Italy. Maybe the whiskey didn't go to a bad cause after all. We had a private party all the way back to Camp Pickett.

Arriving back in camp just in time for reveille, with eyes half open, legs that refused to respond to orders from the brain, we dazedly responded to roll call. It took me about two days to get back completely to my former physical condition. Luckily, the officers weren't in much better shape during this time, so field exercises were less rigorous than normal.

That weekend all leaves were canceled, as the division was to start its last amphibious operation before leaving the States. So it was off to the Virginia coastline where the division embarked on a troop transport that was to take the troops to a landing off the Maryland coast for our final war games. The next time was to be the real McCoy. As the ship sailed up the Virginia coastline, the natural entertainment for troops, card playing and dice, started. While waiting to disembark I got into a game of chance, one I should have left alone. After playing half the night and losing a sizable sum, I swore never to play craps with strangers again.

Having stayed up half the night gambling, I wasn't too awake when I climbed down a rope ladder that was thrown over the side of the ship and into an LCP (landing craft personnel) The cold wind soon woke me up as the boat bumped its way toward shore. When the boat hit the beach, everyone made a dash to get off the beach as instructed. My platoon was to rendezvous at an abandoned hut about five miles inland and help to set up a battalion c.p. (command post). Reaching the house in a little over an hour the c.p. was made functional, but no one arrived from our battalion. Other soldiers from other battalions crowded into the house as it started to snow, which was rather freakish for that time of year. Later it turned to a freezing rain as confusion reigned all over the place, nothing unusual for the army. For a week we lived outside and under combat conditions.

Waiting on the beach to re-embark on the ship that had brought us to this desolate beach, corporals Rerter and Rogo started throwing sand and then ended by throwing the sand down my rifle barrel. Then I grabbed their rifles and filled them with sand. Just then Lieutenant Russo our platoon leader, came by. When he saw that he restricted us all to camp for the next two weeks and that ended my last chance to go home. That is, if I were to get another chance to go home. Boarding the ship we arrived at Camp Pickett without further incident and the next weekend, I was C.Q. (Charge of Quarters) while almost everyone departed from camp.

The following Monday, I was informed that I had been picked to go to chemical warfare school as gas officer for the company. Relieved of my other duties, I spent the next two weeks learning about different gases that might be used by the enemy and the defenses against such attacks.

When I got back to the company, I could feel a certain coolness between Lieutenant Russo and the noncoms from Oklahoma in my platoon. The lieutenant was glad to have me back and handed me all the assignments for the platoon instead of the sergeant, which infuriated the sergeant, and made him madder than ever at me. Walking into the barracks one day, one of the men handed me a leaflet that he said Corporal Rogo was passing around in the barracks that had been sent to him by his girlfriend that lived in New York. It was a scurrilous anti-Semitic leaflet that said "Abie Cohen was the first American to get retread tires while Colin Kelly was the first American to die in combat." That was the first anti-Semitism that I had run into in all the tine I had been in the army.

A number of the men stood around to see my reaction while I read the leaflet. When I finished reading the article, I asked who had brought in this piece of garbage? When told it was Corporal Rogo, I sat and waited for him to come into the barracks. My wait lasted only a few minutes. As Corporal Rogo walked in, I held up the leaflet and solemnly yelled, only a whore who had screwed half of the male population of New York could have sent anything like this through the mail. Corporal Rogo looked at me and kept walking, whereupon I repeated the same phrase I had just uttered. Without a word he walked right out of the building. That was the end of that, but I had called his girl a whore and my response seemed to please everyone, including me, for I had challenged him to come to the defense of his girlfriend's good name, but he didn't take up the gauntlet. He was a good guy and what he thought was a joke had backfired.

In the final weeks of preparation before being shipped out, the activities in the company were reaching a crescendo. Rifle practice for the battalion was next on the list and my platoon was given the job of being in charge of the target area. So from dawn until dusk I was on the rifle range in charge of the target area. We were enclosed in bunkers right beyond and below the targets and had to telephone the scores back to the officers in charge of the men who were firing their rifles. Once in a while, we would get some soldiers who would get all bullseyes, but to take the ego out of them a signal denoting a "Maggies Drawers" (zero, a complete miss) was signified. The phones would ring back always with the words "take another look."

This ploy would always be used with some smart-aleck officer with the most humorous results.

I came back one evening and found out that Lieutenant Russo had been transferred to a rifle company; the Okies had succeeded in getting rid of him. In his place came another lieutenant by the name of Nove. He made the mistake of calling me out to take over the platoon while the sergeant was lined up with the platoon. Apparently the sergeant was to be replaced but that didn't make it easier for me, as the sergeant was still in command when we got back to the barracks.

Two men who had gone A.W.O.L. had come back and had to be brought to the prisoners' cage so the sergeant gave me the detail. It was a 5-mile walk to the prisoners' cage.

The platoon was taken off the rifle range as we had to start packing our equipment and we were given the job of getting the company's baggage assembled. As space was limited all equipment had to be figured in cubic feet and the mathematics was the lieutenant's job. While on another detail, I got a hurry up call to come back to Company Headquarters as the lieutenant wanted to see me. His first question was, "Do you know how to figure in cubic feet?" His embarrassed answer to my "yes" was that he was going to get married that week and he didn't have time to do the work himself and he only had two days to figure the space that the baggage was going to take up in the hold of the ship. He was a typical "90-day wonder" coming from the South who probably brownnosed his way to officers' school; he was pretty ignorant when it came to simple mathematics.

I was left with figuring out the space needed for the equipment while the lieutenant went on his honeymoon. What a difference for an enlisted man; a friend of mine (Dave Cavanaugh) had been promised a furlough to go home to get married, but it was canceled. He went home anyway and when he came back the next week, he told me his company commander wanted to court-martial him for going A.W.O.L. I never did find out what happened, as the next time I saw him was right after the Battle of Salerno and the incident had been completely forgotten by then.

The following week, I was back on the firing range detail. It was getting close to something and the excitement could be felt all over camp. My platoon was put in charge of an obstacle course but this was something different from the regular obstacle course. Two machine guns were set up by the heavy weapons company overlooking a large open field and our job was to put sticks of dynamite in the ground and to explode them as the men went crawling through the field. We had to be especially careful not to explode the dynamite as the men crawled directly over the explosives.

When some of the men heard I was in charge of the explosives, they suddenly became overly friendly, especially the officers. All were trying to find out where the dynamite was positioned in the field. I ran a practicelike run through the combatlike field to see how dangerous it would be and it was like taking one's life in one's hands. The only way to successfully traverse the course was to slither through it like a snake. Knowing where the explosives were hidden was a great help to me but the machine gun bullets flying over my head taught me how to stay close to the ground. I only had to contend with the machine guns, as I knew where the explosives were hidden, but what of the others who had to follow? Was it any wonder that I became so popular?

The final days of our training were approaching. Physical exams were scheduled for the following weekend. Close order drill continued every day with all noncoms put in charge of the company for ten minutes or so each day in order to give them command capability for who knew how many officers would be left to take charge in a combat situation. I was called back to take charge of the detail for the firing range so for the rest of that week that was my duty. On the last day of my detail, when I got back to the barracks all the noncoms and P.F.C.s were sewing stripes onto all their different shirts and Rogo told me to sew on mine if I hadn't already. Here it was 9 P.M. and I had been on special duty. Besides, only my fatigues lacked any stripes. The captain had given orders that any one that didn't have his stripes on all his uniforms would lose them. I thought that my special detail would excuse me for the time being so I didn't heed the warning and went to bed.

The next morning when the company fell out for reveille, everyone was in their fatigues, including me—but my stripes weren't on this uniform. The sergeant was in front of the platoon in his regular position, but the captain called a meeting of all platoon leaders and stood there instead of directing the first sergeant to dismiss the company and walked away as he normally did; whereupon the sergeant called me to the front to take over the platoon.

There I was in full view of the Captain, without stripes on either sleeve. When he saw my stripeless sleeves he ordered me to report to the orderly room after the company was dismissed. I could see a smile on Sergeant Kans's face as I passed him to take over the platoon. After all, he thought I was going to be busted and I was his heir apparent.

In the orderly room, the captain asked me why I hadn't sewn my stripes on my fatigues. My answer was that my detail was on the firing range until almost 9:00 P.M. in charge of the target area and wasn't informed of his order. It had been Sergeant Kans's duty to inform me and he hadn't, so I wasn't lying. The captain told me he had given an order the previous day with the threat to bust anyone who didn't follow that order and he could make no exception. When I walked out of the orderly room, I was a buck private. To blame anyone but myself would be the mark of a sore loser and so I suffered my ignominy in silence.

The first sergeant asked me if I wanted to stay in the same platoon or be transferred to another section: antitank, communications or intelligence. I chose intelligence, like a fool! The work of this unit was to set up observation posts (O.P.s) for the battalion and when not doing this type of work, two men were attached to each rifle company so as to be able to report back to battalion the battle conditions the company was undergoing.

Taking my place in the platoon was a soldier by the name of Bead and as he came out of intelligence, my transfer was easily accomplished. What did he know about explosives, laying barbed wire, bangalore torpedoes (pipe bombs) or other duties of the platoon? Nothing! It made no difference to me, but for those who were looking to succeed me and had the experience it was a disappointment. His main qualification for the job was that he had ridden in one of the cars going to Washington and the captain happened to be in the same one, and I was told that he bitched all the way up and back to the captain that he couldn't get ahead in the company.

One of the men who had been in the car told me about that incident and that was two weeks before I was busted. The captain was on his way to Boston to see his girl friend even though it was rumored he had a wife back in Oklahoma.

All the other companies were having a last beer blowout with funds that were divided up from the profits from the PX and given to all companies of the regiment. But our captain lined up the company and when the men started to bitch about not having a beer party with the funds from the PX, he calmly told the company that he was investing that money in U.S. war bonds in the company's name and we would get the money when we got back. Was he kidding? Who knew if one was still going to be alive to enjoy any of these funds? Either he was stupid or we were completely naive to accept this explanation.

For those men who were over thirty-eight, glad tidings came down from Washington. It was an order to discharge all men thirty-eight or over who wanted to leave the army. It was late May and certainly a good time for anyone to leave the service. Come to think of it, anytime would have been a good time to leave the army.

One of those men over thirty-eight was a soldier by the name of Manrib. He was a pleasant fellow and had been friendly with the first sergeant, but before he left he went around borrowing money from some of the men. He said that he had a pass to go home to New York. He came to me and asked for money, but I told him I knew he wasn't coming back and not to pull that shit with me. What I didn't know was that he had borrowed money from other men in the outfit. A week later when those men who loaned him money found out he had been discharged they came to me because he was of Jewish extraction and they thought I might give them back their loans and somehow get it back from him. Instead of calling them dumb bastards, I told them I had loaned the son of a bitch $100 and I was stuck for a lot more than them. (It was a most embarrassing position as a Jew!)

The physical exams came up the next day and the whole battalion was herded into a large auditorium where the division doctors were busy giving each man a complete physical exam. As each man completed his exam, he was given a card that bore the results, and he was to hand it in as he left the hall. As one of the doctors examined me with his stethoscope, he asked me if I had any difficulty breathing and like a dummy I said, no! He asked the same question again and I gave the same answer. After marking a few symbols on my card, he gave the card to me. After making my way to the rear, I saw Rakos watching another soldier being examined with the greatest interest. The doctor was examining this soldier's feet. When Leone, who was the one examined, came by with his card, Rakos asked to look at it, and when Leone told him the code words on the card were for flat feet, Rakos immediately copied them down on his own card. He then asked me if I wanted to copy the symbols on my card. Again, my principles got in my way. Anyhow, who wanted to miss a free boat ride to Europe?

A few days later, a few of the fellows asked me if I had heard from Rakos. They told me that they had loaned him money to go home and he had promised to send the money back just as soon as he got back to New York. Rakos had been transferred to limited service from our company because of flat feet. He borrowed money from some unsuspecting soldiers with the intention of never returning the money. What was worse, he was Jewish. How could these guys, Rakos and Manrib, do these things? Had they no shame?

The week before we left for our destination, the Okies were busy packing up their suntans and extra shoes to send home. When asked why they would want to wear army clothes if they ever did get back alive from Europe, their answer was that they would have something to wear when they got back. One must remember that more than one pair of pants or shoes was a rarity to many of them so while the Northerners looked on, the Okies packed their extra belongings and mailed them home while the supply sergeant looked the other way.

The division arrived at Camp Patrick Henry about May 26, where we waited to be sent to Hampton Roads, our point of embarkation.

While there, two of the men I had brought to the stockade back for going A.W.O.L. at Camp Pickett, came to me and told me that they were going to take off again and asked me it I would like to join them. I had treated them well and they thought I had been given a raw deal when my stripes were taken away. They had enough confidence in me to think I wouldn't turn them in, which of course I wouldn't. Trying to talk them out of this venture proved unsuccessful and the next that was heard about them was that they had been picked up and ended up in another division, that later went to Italy. Both were killed north of Rome. Thomas and Thompson might have been better off if they had stayed where they were. There was no guarantee that they would have done much better with their original outfit.

My section was ordered to embark at Hampton Roads about a week before the rest of the battalion, as we were to be the advance party. As we walked up the gangplank of the ship with our equipment slung over our backs, we could see the name of the ship: *Florence Nightingale*—the name of a nurse! Was this a good or bad omen? After having been shown our quarters which was one deck down, our section took a walk around the main deck where we encountered some of the sailors who looked at us with awe but kept their distance.

As we looked over the railing of the ship watching the loading crews hoisting jeeps, trucks and other heavy equipment onto the ship, two of the sailors finally walked over to us and with a timid voice one asked, "Are you men commandos?" The silence almost shattered my ears. George Delano gasped. Jiggs Lindner had a stony look. Dupree started to laugh. I visualized pictures of British commandos at Dieppe. How could I be one of those guys? Hitting a beach and overrunning the enemy—that's what commandos do. Wait a minute, that sounds like our training, but that can't be us; we're no commandos! It did give a certain amount of pride to my ego, even though it seemed like a case of mistaken identity.

"What makes you think that we are commandos?" I asked.

The answer quickly came from one of the sailors who had shown us so much respect. "With all the amphibious equipment we hauled on board, what else can you soldiers be?"

Not wanting to lie or lose their respect we walked quietly away and acted as if we didn't have to converse any further.

It was no bargain being the advance party for our company. We had to spend five extra days on the ship waiting for the rest of the battalion to arrive—not even a newspaper to read, something that I regarded as something of a calamity.

There wasn't any lack of card games onboard and I was soon involved in one my second day onboard the ship. The other companies' advance parties consisted mainly of their kitchen crews. We were about the only men who could be considered part of the original landing party, so we were issued long knives or elongated daggers which we stuck into the side of our legging. Sitting down with five strangers in a poker game with a dagger stuck in one's legging gave one extra confidence and this confidence was soon tested.

Having run into a few card cheats in my experiences in the army, the last one in my company with a fellow by the name of Niski who I caught sitting on a fistful of cards and who later chickened out on Anzio with a psycho card and in combat was always making remarks such as, if his name ended in y (inferring that if he were Jewish) he would be out of combat, but I'll get to that later. After playing about a half hour with these strangers I found myself about $100 ahead. There was another soldier who also was quite a bit ahead but we had not up to that time bumped heads with two good card hands. Then it happened. While playing five card stud, my first three cards were jacks. I didn't raise, although this soldier kept raising my jacks.

Keeping my eyes on his bottom card, I kept calling and then noticed an edge of an extra card below his closed card. Then I bet and he raised and I called. He tried to turn over both cards clipped together but I separated the cards, picked up the pot with one hand, pulled my dagger from my legging with the other, and walked away from the game. No one made a move after me but that was the last time I played cards outside of my company.

Finally the rest of the battalion arrived and boarded the ship. It was good to see these men because it was a sign that the ship would be leaving soon, and boredom was taking its toll on my mind. However if there was any way of looking into the future, I would have been glad to have spent the rest of the war on the *Florence Nightingale* tied to the docks at Norfolk, Virginia.

Once loaded, all the ships of the division rendezvoused from Hampton Roads and picked up the naval escort which consisted of cruisers U.S.S. Boise, U.S.S. Brooklyn, and the U.S.S. Philadelphia, and at least eight or more destroyers. The convoy headed east on the morning of June 8, a little more than a month before the division would hit the Sicilian beaches on July 10. Watching the water slip away from the ship as we steamed out of Hampton Roads, a thought came to me: where were all the wild cheering people and bands that one usually saw in war pictures? I didn't even have last week's newspaper. What a sendoff!

The soldiers lined the railings on the ship to watch the destroyers that were running parallel to the ship on either side and at about 50 yards distance. It made quite a scene as one watched the convoy sail east in the late afternoon sun. A thought came to my mind: was this a one-way ticket that had been issued to me or, hopefully, a round-trip ticket to and from the greatest adventure of my life? Our section was bunked one deck down with the other soldiers but off to the side as the intelligence section carried a bit of status and the ordinary chores such as KP and standing guard were eliminated from our duties. This left nothing to do but bathe in the heat of the sun in a semitropical climate on the deck of the ship that was completely covered by the bodies of soldiers sunning themselves. Paperback books were very much in evidence, as whoever was in charge of recreation for the men thought this would be a good way to keep their minds busy, but for me this was a waste of time, as most of the books were detective or mystery stories, better suited for a grammar-school class.

There were innumerable card games and most of these were gin rummy games with small stakes. The games that our company had going were on the deck right in front of the superstructure that contained the officers' mess and as it was in the navy, the mess personnel were all Black. The cooking and baking were done by an open window, thus the smell of freshly baked pies slowly drifted through the window to the nostrils of the soldiers playing cards. Not being able to stand this culinary outrage, I walked over to the open window and asked one of the mess personnel if he was interested in selling one of the pies? His answer was a quick nod of the head and two fingers in the air, which I took to mean two dollars.

Walking back to the card game with a hot lemon pie made me the envy of every GI within smelling distance. Sitting down with the other players, I divided the pie and we made a rule that whoever was ahead had to buy the pies in the future. Some of the other soldiers upon seeing this started going over to the open window and buying pies, as if they were walking into a bakery back home. The next day when I went to get a pie the price had gone up to five dollars; those navy guys learned real fast, but it made no difference. They sold all they could bake. Of course, the officers' share of dessert must have been cut, for I don't know if they found time to bake for the officers' mess.

The gin rummy games continued full blast on the deck of the ship from right after breakfast until early evening with only lunch and supper breaks. The food seemed to get worse the further the ship got into the south Atlantic. The only consolation were the dessert pies at $5 a toss, but who cared about money at this stage of the War?

Cigarettes were 50 cents a carton and nonsmokers soon became smokers. Some of the men couldn't resist the bargain. Two of these men were George Delano and Al Hook. They had never smoked before, and coughed their way through the first four cartons before they became acclimated to the smoke.

The ship continued to zigzag its way across the quiet Atlantic with the destroyers continually dashing around the convoy. The weather got hotter as the ship got closer to Africa, and the food got worse, until finally the main subsistence for me became the hot pies put out by the navy mess personnel who had become instant businessmen.

If I didn't know the direction of the ship was eastward, I might have been fooled into believing that we were traversing the Pacific instead of the northern south Atlantic. The ocean was calm, and the only waves were made by the destroyers that kept running by our ship in both easterly and westerly directions.

One night sitting on deck, I was approached by some members of a platoon who were standing guard on the ship and who I knew well. They asked me to stand guard with them. Laughingly, I told them to blow it out of their posteriors; however, I was intrigued when they only wanted to stand guard against any naval or army officer that might be passing by a walk-in box (big icebox) where many meat-and-cheese delicacies were kept for the officers' mess.

I joined the men voluntarily on their guard duty on the 12 to 8 shift on the upper deck where the officers lived with a bit of civility. My intentions were not to protect the officers but find a new source of food. There was a lock on the walk-in box, but that was no obstacle to two of the men in the platoon. They soon had it picked and as I went inside the walk-in box, a wonderful sight was mine to behold. Hanging at arm's distance were salami, bologna, and all kinds of cheeses. Suddenly the door was slammed shut from the outside. We knew it was done by one of the guards—probably an officer was walking through the area.

About five minutes later the door opened and the sergeant of the guard walked in, explaining that an officer had walked by and he had to slam the door shut. That evening after helping ourselves to some salami and cheese, a battle plan evolved for the future nights on guard. Whenever an officer would be sighted by any one on guard, two knocks on the door of the walk-in box would be given and one knock would signify that all was clear and for those inside to pass out the goodies.

The food really belonged to the American government and where in the constitution does it say that officers are entitled to the best food? We were taking only what belonged to us. Screw the officers! For a week or so, I was able to pass out salami and cheese to a few of my friends, which was a pleasant surprise for them.

One morning I was awakened by a cry that reverberated through the ship. "Land!" Sure enough, the ship was traveling through the Strait of Gibraltar. On one side was North Africa; on the other was Spain with Gibraltar almost close enough to touch. Immediately that old Prudential Insurance advertisement came to mind. "Strong as the Rock of Gibraltar."

Thoughts then came to my mind; how many of these soldiers would be coming back this way? Was this the one and only look at this famous rock for myself? Just then, over the ship's radio over the loudspeaker system came a bulletin from the BBC (British Broadcasting Company) announcing a report from Berlin that an Allied fleet was passing through the Straits of Gibraltar. We were famous. Those German spies in Spain wasted no time in sending back the report that we had been sighted and every Nazi submarine captain was probably on the alert trying to do his best for that Austrian bastard, Hitler. Tangier on the North African side, Gibraltar on the European side—I had become an instant world traveler.

Chapter Three

The Landing in Africa

The ship anchored about 10 miles from Oran in Algiers. Then on June 24 the convoy raised anchor, as we were going to have a last practice amphibious operation before heading for our first combat amphibious engagement. As far as I knew, it wasn't too far up the coast from where we had first anchored.

Around 3 in the morning, we started to disembark from the ship but everything was so confused no one seemed to get into the right LCP. We clambered over the ship's railing and down a rope ladder that was strung alongside of the ship. There were no casualties as the water was serene and the men had taken their amphibious training seriously.

The intelligence section that I was part of, all got into the same LCP though we were assigned to the line company by twos and that was the way we landed on the North African beach. As we hit the beach, troops were moving in all directions and we had to wait for the sun to rise, so we would know if we were headed in the right direction.

Our staging area was about 18 miles west along the coast road and the line of troops that finally wound up on this road was a good indicator that we were headed in the right direction. The hot African sun soon took its toll. Men were stretched out along the roadside worn out by the sun and the wine that they had purchased from the cafes along the way. The sights along the way were an exhilarating experience. Watching Vietnamese prisoners of war who had fought with the Vichy French eating their meal out of community dishes with their hands and flies partaking of their meal as if it had been also served to the flies was enough to turn one's stomach. These Vietnamese or Indonesian troops had fought for the French Vichy government of Petain and now were incarcerated, but in reality they didn't know what they were fighting for, except maybe, for their three meals.

On our own, our section wasn't averse to stopping at one of the cafes run by the French, where the wine tasted as if it had just come out of a vinegar barrel. Feeling the heat and the wine, we stopped to rest along the roadside. Just then our captain came by in a jeep. Seeing us sprawled out under a tree seemed to arouse his anger to a point as if he had just been deprived of his monthly whiskey ration. Threatening us with all kinds of punishment if we didn't catch up with the rest of the battalion, he drove off looking for more stragglers.

Walking along sluggishly and moving from the road only when any vehicles came by, I started to wonder how we could catch up with the rest of the unit. Just then an open command car came by and the driver stopped and asked us if we were going to Oran and to hop in as he would be glad to take us there. Jumping into the vehicle, we all smiled at each other and told the driver to take off. In about ten minutes, we reached the end of the regimental line and as the command car went down the road between the two columns stretched out on each side, I gave a signal to duck as we passed by our battalion. Ten minutes later, we left our regiment behind and then I explained to the driver that our destination was the hills on the south side of the road and showed him the map. Apparently he knew the area and when he came to the cut-off in the road he insisted on driving us up the road to the bivouac area.

Our job had been to get to the bivouac area first so as to direct the battalion En into the right bivouac area. I told the driver to let us off at the crossroad that was pinpointed on our map, as that was where we were supposed to be instead of driving another mile to our camp.

Getting off his command car we properly thanked the driver and pooled about a dozen packs of cigarettes as a gift. Everyone immediately laid down under the trees that were clumped together where the roads came together.

There they were all stretched out: Sam Karp, Ralph Dupree, George Delano, Jiggs Lindner, as if they had covered the 18 or 20 miles by foot. Everyone was awakened from their stupor by a loud shout, "That's the kind of soldiers I want under my command." It was our captain. He didn't stop to think that only two hours earlier and about 15 miles back, he had threatened us with whatever punishment was within his means and here we were. He actually thought we had covered the 15 miles or so by foot in two hours, a typical bird-brained officer and he was smarter than most officers. Of course, he was riding in a jeep up and down the column and probably didn't realize the difference in speed between walking and riding.

The troops of the regiment came slowly up the hill and we directed them to their correct bivouac.

I had started out the morning in a carefree manner. Along the way we had found an officer's mapcase but it was filled with love letters from whomever he had spent the last days with in the States. As we read the letters aloud under the trees to amuse ourselves, the wording got more torrid, such as, "When my tongue glided over your body..." It certainly was most amusing, but the dumb son of a bitch; how could he forget his map case? We weren't even in combat and already one officer had lost his head.

After all the troops of the base had passed, our job was done. Walking the last mile to our camp in a straightforward manner past the troops who were lagging down in the bivouac area, and looking like supermen, we laid down our equipment and promptly set up our tents. I had become a strategist this day and my tactics had paid off.

Guard duty and KP weren't included in our section's labors, so we milled around for the next few days. At night, the serenity of the African night was interrupted by shots fired by the guards on duty at Arabs trying to steal white sheets and anything they could lay their hands on. Most of the hands became dead hands as the soldiers on guard tried to sharpen their rifle skills before they met an enemy that could shoot back.

The last night before we were to board the ship for our final destination, the men were asked to chip in for a few barrels of Algerian wine for our last party before combat. We were told the battalion executive officers had made a good deal on price and it would cost only a few dollars.

The party was on. Wine, or it could have been a high class of vinegar, was passed out to us in our field cups. No cups were enough and walking around the camp watching the soldiers pass out from sour wine wasn't a pleasant sight.

The next morning after reveille, those who could eat breakfast were in line waiting to be fed, and I must admit it was one of the smallest lines I had been in since my army career had started.

Then we were hauled back to the ships on trucks and boarded the *Florence Nightingale* like passengers. We didn't have to clamber back up the side of the ship the way we had left.

It was now July and the ships moved to the harbor of Mers Elkibar, where the ship anchored waiting for further orders.

While anchored with other ships, balloons were flown above. The vessels were used as protection against low-flying enemy planes, and as we sweated out our next move, the Fourth of July had arrived. In celebration of the holiday, an announcement came over the loudspeaker that a special lunch would be served. This special holiday lunch consisted of a Spam sandwich with a hot cup of coffee, just the drink for a temperature of almost a 100 degrees in the shade.

As we sat eating this sumptuous lunch, some sailors came on deck with ice-cold Cokes and ham-and-cheese sandwiches. For dessert they were given ice cream. Here we were going to make an amphibious invasion and were treated like cattle. The Navy, as I was to find out, always fed well, but at fault were those higher up in the Army command who didn't seem to have any consideration for the men who did the fighting.

Going down the stairs to the deck where the sailors had their mess, hoping to grab a sandwich and Coke, I saw a sight that was amusing. There was Morris, our mess sergeant, engaged in a poker game with some sailors. Walking over to the table they were standing around. I nudged Morris and he laughed, for he knew what my light push was for. Those poor sailors were getting cleaned out by Morris and, well, they deserved it, if they couldn't see what he was doing. I didn't get the cold Coke I had come after.

Just then the ship's motors seemed to start, so I went back up the stairs to the open deck just in time to see the ship bang into the side of a destroyer that was anchored alongside of us. Hoping some damage had been done to our ship so we might be taken out of the invasion, we were disappointed for the destroyer's side sustained the damage and was taken away for repairs.

Hook, Delano, and Filosi looked on disparagingly and I wasn't too elated about our misfortune, but then again, hadn't we been awarded a hot cup of coffee in 100 degree weather with a Spam sandwich to celebrate the Fourth of July?

The next day, July 5, we actually moved out of the harbor of Mers El Kibir and moved easterly into the rising sun. As the morning broke into the afternoon, we were on the open sea heading in a north-easterly direction and it seemed as if we were heading for Greece or Crete.

July 6 came and with it the information that the island of Sicily was to be our destination. This easterly course was a ploy to any enemy sighting of the invasion force. They would come to the conclusion that we were headed for some Greek island.

July 7 and most of July 8 we continued to head eastward and then as evening fell the ships turned west in the darkness of the Mediterranean and into a storm that had descended on the fleet. Our ship really hit the high seas and I felt sorry for anyone who was prone to seasickness.

The preceding day, a speech given by Winston Churchill, came over our loudspeaker system from BBC radio and one line I shall always remember, "There will be action in the Mediterranean before the leaves of Autumn fall." How prophetic! That line remained in my mind as we headed through the stormy seas for Sicily on July 9 with the little corvette or subchasers racing alongside our ship, half submerged in the water as wave after wave swept completely over their decks.

Chapter Four

Sicily: First Combat

Early in the evening of July 9, the ship started to slow down and everyone was alerted to be ready in a few hours to take their positions on the upper deck, where the rope ladders were to be hung over the side of the *Florence Nightingale*. The seas were still rough as the ship came to a halt and anchored.

Below deck, the men were being served their last snack—a Spam sandwich with a sour pickle—just the thing for anyone with an upset stomach on a stormy sea.

As the loudspeaker rang out our orders to assemble on deck, the men started climbing the stairs, and the ship was rolling and heaving so strongly that a few soldiers fell down the stairs and just laid there moaning. Whether it was a ruse or for real I didn't know, but how lucky can one get, to be injured before the invasion?

On deck, I watched an intriguing scene as the Navy was loading Army vehicles by bringing them from below decks on a winch and loading them into waiting landing ships. The jeeps swung to and fro across the ship as the sailors, mooring the winch tried to lower the vehicles into the waiting landing craft. This was certainly a hazardous job. Into one of the jeeps went one of the drivers who wanted to go aboard the landing craft with his jeep. What a mistake! The jeep turned upside down and in every direction as the ship rolled in the high seas. The driver, who was of Indian ancestry, rode the jeep like a cowboy on a wild horse for about thirty minutes. It looked like he might let go of the winch and come crashing to the deck.

While this scene was going on, flashes in the sky denoted that antiaircraft fire was being directed at planes flying overhead. It was later learned that our own Navy was firing at our own planes going to Sicily to unload soldiers of the 82nd Airborne Division. While those fireworks were going on, there was a light coming from shore.It first beamed into the sky and then swept across the water, but failed to pick anything out of the water as there was no return fire from the batteries onshore. Then more flashes came from shore as our planes bombed the area and destroyers ran close to the coastline to fire salvo after salvo into the area where the enemy was supposed to be. While this went on for about an hour or so, word came to start leading the LCPs.

As I climbed over the side of the ship onto the rope ladder, I held on tightly as the ship continued to heave wildly; the darkness didn't help. As I touched the floor of the LCP, I waited for it to come up to me, the way I was trained, and then dropped onto the ship. I could feel the floor go down with the heaving seas.As I got both feet sliding on the floor I let go of the ladder. Just then the ship dropped about 10 feet; luckily, no one got hurt on our ship.

The LCPs circled for about an hour. After rendezvousing for about an hour, the ships drove for shore. It was a little after 4:00 A.M. when we hit the beach, running out of the LCP right onto sand. Other ships had unloaded in the water. We were able to run ashore, until we were about 50 yards inland, where other troops were hiding behind a small sandy hill.

No one moved out; apparently the men in charge were waiting for it to get a little lighter. As we grouped around, a lieutenant from another company came by and demanded that some soldiers go with him to pull his jeep out of the sand. We had a job to do and that wasn't to pull his jeep out of the sand. He then threatened to court-martial us, and the only answer he got was a soft laugh from the group waiting to move out.

Delano, Lindra, and I moved out over the sand dunes and onto the hilly ground; we were supposed to contact the line companies and as I climbed one of the dunes to see where we were, daybreak was at hand. I could make out the outline of the area. Just then tracer bullets flew over my head from a machine gun on our right rear which we apparently had passed in the late darkness of the morning. Rolling down the sand dune at the glimpse of the tracers above my head, I thought how lucky it was that the enemy was such a bad shot! After wiping the sand from my rifle and myself, I started to call myself names for exposing myself on top of a sand dune for all the enemy to see.

Advancing around the sand dunes we started heading inland when we heard the motor of a plane. Looking up I could see the pilot of the German Messerschmidt looking right down on us. I still don't know why I didn't take a shot at him; that's how close he was overhead. Looking down on us, he probably didn't know whether we were Germans or not, as our helmets were similar. The plane continued to fly down toward the beach which the enemy plane started to strafe.

What a fool I had been! There was a chance to shoot down an enemy plane and I missed it. I was still green and had the courage to face enemy planes. As experiences caught up with me, the nearest ditch was a mark of my courage at the sound of an enemy plane overhead.

As we looked over our maps trying to figure the way to the town of Victoria, almost on a direct line from Scoglitti on the coast, two miles from the communication section Sergeant Stout and Sergeant Bering came to us for aid in carrying their roll of wire. It was strung out back to battalion headquarters wherever that was at that time. Bering was crying and Stout wanted someone to carry Berring's end of the roll of wire. That was the second time I saw a soldier crying. The day before the landing, Rerter came crying to me complaining that he was supposed to go ashore as a frogman to put signal lights on the shore before the invasion started. I asked him why he had volunteered to go to Florida to train as a frogman. The only answer was tears. He was lucky; the Navy frogmen were the only ones used.

As we casually proceeded down the road with houses scattered alongside, no one seemed to be aware that there was a war going on. Coming to a crossroad, we came upon eight paratroopers from the 82nd Airborne Division. They had a 75-mm artillery piece set up guarding the road.

They had jumped that night and set up a roadblock at the crossroad. It was a wonder how they got their artillery piece set up. A bigger wonder was that our Nary hadn't shot them down.

Asking them to join us on the way to Vittoria, a quick refusal was the answer, since they were supposed to guard the crossroads. They were smarter than we; there were only six of us and we were headed for the town ahead of the line companies until Delano shouted out to wait for some more troops before proceeding, a really smart move.

L Company moved up and we joined them as they made their way into Vittoria. Then sniper shots rang out and a few wounded was the result of inexperience. The town was taken and so ended our first day of combat.

The next day the battalion started out to take the Comiso Airport; only this time everyone had taken their rightful position. Delano and I were attached to I Company and as we moved along the road, I found myself traveling with the men in the company point where I had no business being and we were caught in a crossfire of two machine guns manned by Germans. As inexperienced as the point men were, they succeeded in knocking out the machine guns.

Coming out of a wooded area, the airport came into full view. Artillery shells were exploding all over the landing field and German planes were trying to take off in the face of the continuous explosion of artillery shells and rifle fire. A few made it—very few.

Pulling out my field glasses to get a better look at the planes, I was mistaken for a sniper by men from another company as they passed by asking how the hunting was. Looks sure are deceiving, but I relished the compliment.

The fighting was still going on as our battalion continued to move north past the airfield and past a minefield that was clearly marked with German signs (Minnen) and a skull and bones. This ended the second day in combat.

The third day, I. was back traveling with my own company when the line was held up by snipers and our section got a quick call to lend help to the troops tied down by sniper fire. Crouching low and moving along the road in single file, we passed the troops lining the ditches watching us go by and giving a big wave and smile as we passed. Getting to the front of the line, sniper fire hit us from all sides, so down everyone went clinging to a stone wall alongside the road. We lay there for about ten minutes, but what seemed like hours. Then Lindner yelled out that he was going to try to make it to a stone house across the road; whereupon, I hit Julie Karp who was laying in front of me. He failed to respond. Thinking he was hit I shook him again and he sleepily looked around. He had fallen asleep in the hot sun. We didn't knock out any snipers, but we managed to make it safely to the stone house, only because the snipers had moved out.

The battalion continued on and again we were tied down, this time by an Italian coast artillery piece that kept whistling shells all around us. That was the first time I felt fear from artillery as the sweat just rolled down my face, this time lying in the shade.

The next day I was attached to I Company right behind K Company, which was the point company. As K Company rounded a bend in the road shots rang out from a Tommy gun. We wondered who was shooting. There were two Italian soldiers bleeding in the road. They had been shot by the company captain when they came to surrender, poor bastards. The captain's brother had been killed on D-Day and the captain wasn't taking any prisoners. It was a sorry sight, but the company walked right by them. Even the battalion colonel who was walking between K Company and I Company walked by. He continued without so much as moving his head. I saw the shooting of the prisoners, but there was a story that an MP sergeant had shot a whole truckload of German prisoners the day before. This was war at its sorriest.

The next morning the battalion was in a defensive position and I was sleeping with I Company when the Germans attacked with tanks and machine guns and mortars. As I lay behind a tree firing, a sergeant from L Company rose and led a charge of his company, overrunning the advancing Germans. What guts! Then for the first time, I saw a chemical battalion in action opening up with their chemical mortars. They fired their burning shells into the German lines. Screams emitted from the mouths of the fleeing Germans as the phosphorous shrapnel fell among them. Tanks appeared on our left flank and some GIs just stood up with their grenade launchers knocking out the tanks. The battle was over in an hour. The battalion rested in that area for the rest of the day and the next morning we were trucked to another area further west. The rumor was that this section was being taken over by the British 8th Army. At that time, fighting alongside the famous 8th Army under Montgomery was like playing in the same baseball league with the New York Yankees, especially to those in combat for the first time.

The next day we detrucked and started the long march up the center of the island of Sicily. After walking about five miles without any opposition, the battalion took a short break. Getting up on a short knoll, Delano and I stretched out to rest. We were still traveling with I Company. While we were relaxing, a truck from our company came up the road with the AP platoon aboard. I yelled to them that this was the front line and they had better stop. They yelled back that they were supposed to set up the battalion CP (command post). I told them not to go any further up the road than the next turn, which they did, as well, there on the side of the hill. About ten minutes later a jeep came tearing up the road with Sergeant Ranks. This driver asked some of the men from I Company if they had seen the AP truck. The men told them that it had just passed up the road. Before anyone could tell them to go no further than the bend in the road, the jeep took off.

About three minutes later, machine-gun fire could be heard around the bend in the road. Everyone soon got up from their relaxed positions expecting some kind of enemy action. But instead, around the bend came the driver of the jeep running as if he were in an Olympic sprint, blood dripping from his arms.

Quickly, the men descended from the side of the hill to ask him what had happened. As the medics gave him emergency treatment, Larry said that he had driven in to the arms of a German tank Mark VI and its machine gun had opened fire hitting him. Running for his life he managed to make it to the bend in the road and back to our position. As he was driven away he said Sergeant Ranks was still out there. He had taken off in such a hurry that he hadn't seen what had happened to the sergeant.

About two minutes after this incident while we just had time to lay down, up the road came our company captain in his jeep. Stopping his jeep right below us while we were out of sight, he started asking for Gershowitz and Delano and whoever he could get to look for Sergeant Ranks.

Now the captain had busted me to private and Sergeant Ranks, back in the States, always implied I was trying to get his job, so why should I put my life on the line for this bozo, I thought. The captain kept yelling my name. Finally I raised my body and went down to where he was sitting in his jeep. He said, "Let's go find Sergeant Ranks," while tears were coming from his eyes. This was one of his men and he hadn't been in combat long enough to get used to men missing in action.

He wanted a patrol to go out to look for Sergeant Ranks. Down from the other side came Karp and Lindner and along with the captain, Delano and me. We moved up the road cautiously. As we came to the bend in the road, we spread out at 25-yard distances. In this formation, we scoured the area where the tank was supposed to be. Luckily for us, the tank was gone and there was no Sergeant Ranks—maybe he had been taken prisoner. (Six months later we learned he had been captured and was a prisoner in Germany.)

What would have happened if we had made contact with the tank? Not one or us had a grenade launcher or bazooka. That's what green in combat really means.

As we headed back to our original position, the battalion started to move forward and met us before we returned to the bend in the road. The captain was really appreciative of our going with him, and it did show he had concern for his men.

Joining I Company again, the column moved up the road about five miles where a small village came into sight. Before the company could move any further a German tank came out from a clump of trees and opened up with its 88-mm artillery piece. Hitting the flat ground was slight protection. There were no ditches to crawl into, and as the shells continued to fall, my fingers started to dig a foxhole automatically.

Someone yelled to bring up our tanks, but the only vehicle to show up was a half-truck with a 75-mm artillery piece.. This was what we called a TD (tank destroyer). I don't know who was more erratic—the Germans in their tank or the man in the TD. As we lay between these two demons of war, the Mark VI opened up with tracer shells trying to line up the TD, but they went about 20 feet above the tank destroyer. Likewise the Americans in the TD were firing with the same kind of accuracy.

After firing at each other for about 10 minutes (it seemed like a week), the German tank withdrew, and I stopped digging with my fingers.

As the battalion moved on the village, one company moved through the town while the other two companies flanked the town on each side. Experience is a good teacher, and the men in charge had learned a lesson at Vittoria, where the battalion had walked into sniper fire. Continuing to move, the battalion went for about another 10 miles that day with no more opposition, so when we lay down that night everyone was practically worn out.

That evening more rations were brought up by the mess sergeant who told us that Duplea had been wounded the day before and who had been evacuated from Sicily. What a lucky dog. We had often talked about getting a million-dollar wound and getting out of combat. I never saw him again. We had paled around in the States; in fact,

I had recommended him for corporal but it had been given to Hogan who was wounded at Salerno.

The next morning the battalion was alerted about 5:00 A.M. to get ready to move out. While grabbing a K ration for breakfast a battery of 105 artillery units came up and set up their guns in support of our advance. I had never seen artillery come up so close to the infantry in my seven days of combat. The men of the artillery unit unloaded their shells and than each gun took a turn firing. I asked the artillery captain why the guns each fired one shot; he replied that the guns were zeroing in on a target on the map which was supposed to be a crossroad.

Moving with K company this time, we were the point company. There was no opposition as we moved in two lines on each side of an old country road. The pace was fairly rapid. About five miles up the road, one could hear yelling and screaming coming from the direction of an old farmhouse; I felt ashamed. Its roof had a gap in it made by a shell, and the people were screaming in Italian "Why?" A few civilians had been killed earlier that day in the house from the artillery that had zeroed in on the crossroad. The civilians kept yelling and screaming at us as we passed by, claiming there was and had not been any enemy there. One could say, "C'est le guerre," but one could also say the artillery should have known where its shells were landing.

A few more miles up the road we came to the city of Caltanisetta which had been used for a supply center by the enemy. Most of the buildings had been destroyed by air raids. The stench was so bad, I couldn't wait to get through the town.

Once through Caltanisetta we were put on trucks and moved further up to the north central part of Sicily and into a hillier area than we had been in.

The battalion was bivouacked around a hill on which our section established an OP (observation post). We were alone and separated from the rest of the battalion. That night the lights started to spring up from the villages in the valley below. We had been under the impression that there was supposed to be a total blackout, or didn't the Sicilians know there was a war on? We were thinking German troops were down in the valley and the blinking lights in the villages were signals. It was reported to the battalion CP that there was unusual activity down in the valley. When no one from battalion was sent up to investigate, the calls were constantly sent back. Until the battalion finally was exasperated and sent up Captain Boggs and the whole of K Company as a precautionary measure. Captain Boggs was furious, as well he ought to be. His company was on the go all day and when they finally had a chance to get some rest, they were alerted to come up the hill in case of an early German attack.

After hanging around for about an hour, watching the lights in the valley going on and off, Captain Boggs figured we had been foolish and ordered his company to leave the hill and take their regular position at its base and go back to sleep. He was so mad he would have shot the six of us at the least provocation. (Captain Bex was an outstanding combat officer despite his gruff manner. He was killed at Salerno.)

Everyone stayed awake until about 4:00 A.M. and then suddenly everyone was sleeping. About 6:00, we were awakened by the section sergeant who had come up from battalion headquarters to pick two men to go with L Company on an advance to the next village that was located on what seemed to be a mountain. We drew cards and Delano and Lindner lost, so off they went with L Company. We could watch the whole procession from our field place as the company slowly found its way up the side of the mountain, with everyone waiting for an attack from the Germans from the top of the mountain.

The mountain was about 12 miles from our OP. Every movement of our men could be observed from our position. Luckily, there was no enemy opposition; otherwise, L Company could have been wiped out.

As soon as L Company reached Castel di Lucia, the village at the top of the mountain, we were alerted to move out at a brisk pace. The battalion reached the mountain village in about three hours.

As we got to the village on the mountain, darkness started to fall. Before the company could get settled a stink-dive bomber came out of the darkening sky and seemed to dive straight for the church steeple.It dropped a couple of bombs hitting somewhere in the village. The mountain shook from the impact. For the next hour, the air attack continued making it seem as if the mountain had been in a continuous earthquake. The villagers had locked all doors in their stone houses, and the soldiers in our company lay on cobblestones in front of the church in this medieval village. The soldiers shook not only from the bomb blasts but from the fear that goes along with them. Finally the air raid was over; everyone just fell asleep from exhaustion.

The next morning Karp and I were sent out to make contact with a 1st Division patrol that was coming up on our right flank. Upon leaving Castel Di Lucia we set out along a mountain pass and on turning a bend in the road came upon an unusual sight. There on a high ridge overlooking the roads for miles was a mountain. Below the mountain was a one-star general, one colonel, one lieutenant-colonel and a major setting up an artillery OP (observations post). It was General McLain, our artillery general. What the hell was a general doing way out on a OP?

General McLain gave us a short snappy salute as we walked by in utter amazement, watching a general do a job that was 2nd lieutenant's work with a staff sergeant or two. I guess the general thought the location of the OP was too important for anyone but himself to handle. (He later became a lieutenant general and corps commander in France).

Walking a few miles along the plateau we ran into the patrol of the first division and after exchanging intelligence, we got back to our lines by early afternoon. Then the whole battalion continued to move forward to the position we had just left.

Delano and I were told to contact a patrol of I Company that had crossed this area after we had left in the morning to see why they had not reported back.

Advancing westward for about a half hour, a house suddenly appeared from beyond some olive trees. There was the patrol with glasses of wine in their hands laying all around the house in an ecstatic mood. Telling then that they were long overdue back at their company headquarters, they ignored what we said. It was getting dark so Delano and I decided to stay around for a while and the old woman of the house was most hospitable with her wine and cheese. A few of the soldiers were of Italian extraction. This made the conversation between the natives and the soldiers no obstacle at all.

As more wine was consumed, the men seemed to get sleepier and soon all were sleeping. This was a mistake which could have been fatal if the enemy had been in the vicinity.

Waking up the next morning, loud. noises emanated from the pathway near the house. The pathway had become an irregular road and the noise were the boots of the soldiers from the battalion. We were supposed to report back to give the details of the area, and here we were sleeping out in enemy territory.

We left the house and joined the battalion as it headed toward Mistretta which was to be our last combat in Sicily.

Mistretta fell with hardly any opposition. Upon joining the company, our captain was happy to see us. He thought we had been killed or captured when we didn't come back that night. I told him that darkness had fallen and that we didn't want to get shot by our own men trying to get back to our lines. That worked and so exploring through Mistretta became the next job, as well as meeting many Sicilians who all seemed to have a cousin in Brooklyn. However, their hospitality was sincere.

The troops were loaded on trucks and we were moved along mountainous roads downhill to where one could see the blue water of the Mediterranean Sea.

As we rode along the twisting roads, it became apparent that the drivers of the trucks were more dangerous than the enemy. They sometimes accelerated the vehicle around curves, where we could look down and not see bottom. This truck battalion seemed like it was going to do what the enemy couldn't do. Fortunately the K rations contained not only cigarettes, but toilet paper as well.

Arriving at our bivouac area near Cefalu, camp was immediately set up. It wasn't that much more comfortable than when we were in combat, but we slept in small tents or on the open ground. Food was made by the kitchen—no more K rations with their artificial sour lemonade and instant coffee that was dropped into a hot canteen. Ice was brought into camp from Palermo and iced tea and coffee were a welcome treats. Hot bread was made by the cooks in our kitchen, so things were looking up—especially with a swim everyday in the Mediterranean Sea.

The battalion had been bivouacked along the seacoast west of Cefelu. The soft blue water of the Mediterranean was about a hundred yards below the sand dunes where the OP had been located, thus giving those on duty at the OP a view for a few miles into the Mediterranean where enemy planes or ships could be observed if any came into this area.

As I lay there looking through the scope at the water and then at the troops bathing for the first time in almost three weeks in the warm water of the ancient sea, my mind wandered back to July 10 when we had disembarked from the *Florence Nightingale*. How foolish the army had been by making the invasion uniform our ODs (dress uniform)! All troops since ancient time wore their best uniforms into battle, but in these times the modern troops were neither in the army as professional soldiers, or regarded themselves as models for the latest thing in uniforms.

To make it more ridiculous hitting a beach in Sicily in 90 degree heat wearing woolens could only be attributed to some dumb general in S4 (supply) who probably was wearing suntans (summer uniform). Luckily for me, I had picked up two outfits worn by officers that looked like our ODs; only they weren't wool. I was allergic to wool, and broke out in a rash and scratched all over the place when I had to wear this wool outfit. So when our barracks bags arrived at this rest area, I was able to change after three weeks and get the other outfit washed.

Another incident sticks out in my mind. It happened on the third night in Sicily. I came close to being shot by our own men. A prisoner had been captured and no one had been able to interrogate him because there were no German-speaking soldiers in battalion intelligence, so someone thought of me as I seemed to give the impression of knowing a little of everything.

A Lieutenant Bond was in command of battalion intelligence and he asked me if I could converse with the prisoner. I used my best Yiddish to ask him who he was and where he came from. His German was almost as bad as my Yiddish. He claimed he was Polish and had joined the German army to get shoes and food. He also claimed to be with the Herman Göering Division. That was the story Italian prisoners used and from looking at their condition, the story of a Polish Nazi using that line was abominable. I might have shot him then and there but for the lieutenant being there. The lieutenant told me to take him back to a prison enclave run by the MPs (military police) a few miles down the road. He called his driver, Frank Bacus, to put the jeep at my disposal.

Pointing to the hood of the jeep, I told the prisoner to sit on it and off the three of us went into the darkness of the night. About a mile down the road two paratroopers from the 82 Airborne stepped out of the shadows and waved to us to stop. After a minute of exchanging amenities, they asked where the prisoner was being take. We told them. "We'll take him off your hands," one of them said, "and shoot the bastard. Do you know," he continued, "that the German bastards caught some of our fellow paratroopers and burned them in oil, and shot our fellow paratroopers when they landed and didn't take them prisoners? We want this son of a bitch. We're going to shoot the bastard." With these words they proceeded to put their hands on him to drag him off the hood of the jeep. At first I thought let then take the Nazi-Polish bastard, but my orders were to deliver him to the MP prisoner enclave. I ordered the paratroopers to get back. With that they raised their Tommy guns and pointed them at Bacus and me. Raising my M-1 rifle, I again ordered them to back off. This was a confrontation that American soldiers would get killed trying to save a Nazi Polish bastard from getting killed.

Thinking fast before any shots went off, I yelled at the paratroopers that as a Jew I had more right to kill the prisoner than they, and that the prisoner would probably shoot me down if I was his prisoner, especially when he had seen my dog tags with the H.

For a minute they hesitated. With that I yelled at Bacus to take off, which he promptly did. I left the paratroopers standing in the road thinking of what I had told them—that they were free to take the prisoner away from the MPs after I had delivered him.

Dumping the prisoner off at the prison enclave, Bacus breathed a sigh of relief and said he wasn't going to drive me with any more prisoners. He had enough to worry about the enemy without getting in arguments with our own troops.

Then I thought about the evening of the invasion when I glanced into the mess hall of the Navy men and saw them eating a buffet of all kinds of cold cuts, salads with fresh lettuce, tomatoes, and cucumbers, while we were feasting on Spam sandwiches. I walked into the Navy mess with my shirt off so as to look like a sailor, and I started helping myself when some other soldiers spotted me. They ran into the Navy mess. Before long there were more army men in there than sailors, and that's when we all got kicked out.

In the evening, coming down from the OP, I would walk over to the communication section and listen to the BBC on their radio. War news was broadcast at six o'clock. Listening usually were the battalion colonel and executive officers, plus a couple of captains and dozens of enlisted men. When the Russians were advancing or when the British or American air forces were bombing the Germans there would be smiles, but if there were any German successes, scowls would appear.

CHAPTER FIVE

Back to Africa

One morning upon awakening my whole body seemed to be burning up. Hardly able to move, I went over to the Lister Bioglong to get some water, but I couldn't quite reach it. Some one called the medics and they carried me over to the battalion aid station where my temperature was taken. Someone said I had malaria; then I was brought some quinine to try to alleviate my condition. Then, half dazed, I was carried in a stretcher to an airplane, which I later found out was a C-47 transport plane. The next thing I knew when I woke up, on glancing through a window near where I was laying, I could see the water below us which didn't seem any more than 50 yards away.

When I awoke, there were stretchers all around on an open field and nurses were walking among us checking temperatures. We were loaded into ambulances and brought to a hospital where I lay for about three days, listless and not knowing what was going on.

When I had gotten back my senses, one of the nurses told me that this was Tunis in Africa, but I didn't care where I was. The bed sheets were like paradise and when I went out in pajamas and a bathrobe to eat, it was a beautiful feeling after crawling around in the hot Sicilian sun for almost three weeks.

Still feeling weak after being in the hospital for about eight days, my activities were limited to feeding myself through a chow line and reading the *Stars & Stripes*, listening to the news and every evening around midnight being awakened by air raids over Tunis by German bombers who seemed to set something on fire in the Tunis area. The hospital was situated on a hill about 15 miles from Tunis and this afforded a front-line seat of the bombings and for a change I was a spectator, not a participant.

As this second week of a welcome enforced vacation was coming to a close, some of us in the ward were allowed to go into the recreation room, play cards, read, or just enjoy being left alone. One day some Red Cross workers came in and asked if there was anything we wanted. Of course, the one answer was cigarettes, as everyone was starting to feel better. Even the nurses, as homely as they were, took on an appetizing flavor.

A carton of cigarettes was given to each soldier after he signed a piece of paper declaring he would pay back the price of the cigarettes to the Red Cross. I signed the paper, but I never forgave the Red Cross. They got millions in donations to buy cigarettes and other things for the soldiers. Demanding to be paid back by combat soldiers for a carton of cigarettes, to me was an act of treason.

As soon as the cigarettes were received, card games erupted all over the recreation hall. I got into a casino game where the stakes of a pack of cigarettes for each 21-point game with four players.

After about two days, there were four cartons of cigarettes under my pillow. Now that I was feeling much better after almost three weeks at the hospital, restlessness seemed to overtake me and as some of the men attached to the medical unit came back with stories of Tunis, I desired to see the sights of this city. Our uniforms had been washed, cleaned, and put in back of our beds as some of us were to be discharged and sent back to our units.

I had met another soldier in the hospital from our regiment who was attached to the regimental band; we had served together in training camp at Camp Cross in the same machine-gun company. His name was Ervin. He was Portuguese, and a hell of a friendly fellow and a desirable companion to explore Tunis with. He had been wounded in Sicily, and the experience had left him quite nervous. His job had been a GRS (grave registration section). They picked up the dead GIs on the front and brought them back to be buried in the rear.

So on a midweek day Ervin and I snuck out of the hospital after breakfast and headed down the road to Tunis. Under my arm were three cartons of cigarettes to be used to trade for whatever they would bring, as money was something that the both of us lacked. The first truck going by picked us up and we were on our way.

As some of the signs went by, my eyes opened wide. Could that sign that we had just passed be right? It read Carthage and pointed in the direction we were headed. Yes, of course, Carthage was near Tunis, or what was left of Carthage. Across my mind filtered glimpses of Hannibal crossing the Alps. "Fool," I said to myself. "The army has given you a free trip back in time. Your ancient history class wasn't for nothing." The truck passed half-destroyed homes and monuments that had to run a couple of thousand years back. Carthage was the home of the Carthaginians, a people I had admired in my ancient history and Latin classes, as the most gallant of warriors. How come with so little to do, the army hadn't made a tourist sight of Carthage for its men? "Don't be a fool," I thought. "Most of the soldiers hadn't even heard of Africa let alone Carthage."

The screeching brakes of the truck brought me out of my dreams of 100 B.C. and into the twentieth century. "Here's the middle of Tunis," shouted the driver, and with that Ervin and I jumped out of the truck and headed into the main area of Tunis.

All signs were in French, and as we started down the street with my cartons of cigarettes, some unusual attention was given to us by the civilian population. The first offer for the cigarettes was 100 francs for a carton, about 5 dollars. A franc then was equal to about 5 cents. "Sold," I said but no sooner than these words were uttered I knew a mistake had been made. Someone shouted 150 francs and then 200. Pulling back the first carton of cigarettes from an irate French man, I yelled, "A bottle of cognac for a carton." Immediately a civilian rushed out of a cafe with a bottle of three-star Hennessy cognac. We sold off the other carton for 310 francs. Left with one carton, off we went to explore the city. In one movie house, Gary Cooper was playing in *Sergeant York*, a World War I picture that I had seen before I was in the army. Women were walking all over the streets with soldiers from all nations. Walking along, someone tapped me on the shoulder. Turning around, I came face to face with a lieutenant who immediately put out his hand and said, "I see you're with the 45th Division. Your outfit did a wonderful job in Sicily." He told me he had served with the division in the States. He introduced us to the other lieutenant with him, saying it was an honor to meet up with two men from the 45th and asked if he could he do anything for us. He told us to take a quick look at the Casbah, but not to linger there after dark as a few GIs had their throats slit. Saying our good-byes and making our way to the Casbah, we passed a synagogue. All I had seen were bombed churches that were still standing, but no synagogues. I thought there must be Jews here, so I walked over to the synagogue, where an elderly man was standing. Speaking to him in English brought no response.

"Parlez-vous Français?" he asked.

"Non," I replied. "Sprachen ze Deutch?" I asked.

"A bissel," he answered.

"Yiddish?" I asked.

He nodded his head. So a conversation in Yiddish began. He told me the history of the synagogue and that there were a number of European Jews who had escaped to Tunis and were saved from the Vichy French by the Americans.

After a tour of the synagogue, I handed him a couple of packs of cigarettes and a 100 francs for the synagogue and left him pointing the way to the Casbah. Strolling along toward the Casbah, thoughts came to my mind of a picture that had come out a few years earlier starring Hedy Lamarr called *The Casbah*. Would this place be as mysterious and dangerous as the Casbah pictured in the movie? Its locale was Algiers, and not Tunis, but I suppose all Casbahs are the same.

Arriving at the entrance, we walked through a slender opening and came upon people milling all over the narrow streets.There were women with veils ogling each foreign person, and small stalls where merchants haggled their wares with prospective customers. It was like walking into the Middle Ages; everything looked so primitive. Having been warned about going too deep into this area because of the criminal element that hid out here, Ervin and I proceeded cautiously down the center of the Casbah. Seeing a man dressed in Western clothes, I walked over to strike up a conversation with him. As he spoke Arabic and French but no English, I was left to my device, German in the form of Yiddish. Again success was with me, as he was Jewish and he lived in the Casbah with relatives, whom he immediately wanted us to meet. He asked me if I 'had ever been to a Bar Mitzvah, Oriental style. Of course, my answer was no. "Come with me," he said. "These people will be glad to see a Jewish soldier from America." So along we went down narrow alleys to a stone house that was situated over a stall that was closed. We followed the gentleman upstairs. As we approached the third and top floor we could hear Oriental music and singing coming out of one of the room. Tambourines, drums, and some instruments I had never seen before made up this Oriental band. We were welcomed with open arms, when it was explained that I was Hebrew. This Bar Mitzvah was one I had never seen. The music was so Oriental that I expected a belly dancer to appear at any moment. Having partaken of some wonderful mideastern hors d'oeuvres that consisted of dates and figs, and an Oriental wine, soon my head was twirling as fast as the people dancing around the room. As it was starting to get dark outside, discretion became the better part of valor, so bidding everyone good-bye and handing over my last 50 francs and three packs of cigarettes as a gift, we were led safely out of the Casbah by the gentleman that had brought us to the party.

Getting back to camp was our next objective, so we went back to the center of town so we could find the signs depicting the way back. Walking along the street, we decided to get a last drink. We traded the last two packs of cigarettes for a small bottle of cognac. We then walked along the road, drinking and waving at every army truck that went by, trying to get a ride back to camp. Finally, a truck stopped. It was already full of GIs no more sober than we were; even the driver had a hard time making his words sound understandable. But the main purpose was to get back to the hospital before anyone missed us, so with the help of the weaving soldiers already on the truck, we were pulled into the vehicle as it started moving.

Though one couldn't see the roadside, the erratic movement of the truck along the bumpy road was enough to let one know that the driver was going at an excessive speed. The truck continued along for a few miles in this manner while the semisober GIs sang whatever songs of back home that came to their minds. Suddenly I felt myself flying through the air. The truck had turned over on a curve. A truckful of GIs were sprawled all over the landscape with more confusion than if an enemy shell had fallen among us.

Maybe it was a good thing that being quite a bit intoxicated, the pain of hitting the ground from an overturned truck was slow to reach my senses. How long the accident victims lay there before ambulances arrived was something I'll never know. I woke up the next morning in my hospital bed, clothed in Army pajamas. Trying to get up, I was unable to move as my bones felt sore all over. I asked one of the medics who attended the ward as substitutes for the nurses what had happened. He said that the driver of the truck was drunk and overturned on a curve while traveling at an excessive speed and I was lucky because the doctors hadn't found any broken bones. Most of the other GIs in the truck had ended up with broken arms or legs. He told me I was due for another examination in the afternoon and would I be able to get up. "Of course not," I answered. "I'm so sore my tongue hurts when I talk."

That afternoon I was carried into the area where the doctors examined the patients. After being examined, the doctor told me, "No broken bones, but you have bronchial asthma." Just then the commander of the hospital, a doctor who was a full colonel, walked into let me know that I would be restricted to the hospital ward until I was to be shipped back to my unit. He would recommend a court-martial for me and all the GIs who had left the hospital without permission for an outing in Tunis.

For three days I was hardly able to leave the bed except to use the latrine, which wasn't often as my appetite had taken a vacation. After the fourth day of practically being confined to the bed, I was able to move my arms and legs without too much pain. So to the chow line I went, as my appetite had returned with a vengeance.

Going through the chow line, the Italian prisoners of war who did the serving, acted as if they were paying for the food. Not having eaten much for three days my appetite had become ravenous. Berating the Italian prisoners for not putting more on my plate, I warned them that they wouldn't be serving food much longer as it would be pretty hard to dole out these portions with broken arms.

It was a week since the accident when an alert was sounded in our ward that all personnel able to move would be immediately sent back to their units. It was almost a month that I had been away from my unit and the end of August was approaching. Yet as I put my clothes on, memories of this place weren't too bad: relaxing in a bed with white sheets, eating hot food every day, listening to the news broadcasts, and reading whatever was available. These are simple things to most people, but to me after almost three weeks in combat in Sicily, it was as if I was a millionaire who had retired to some estate in France.

The next day after breakfast, two truckloads of GIs were trucked from the hospital to the harbor of Tunis where an army embarkation point had been set up to load the GIs returning to their units in Sicily. Everyone was given three K rations for the trip and the only smokes were in the K rations. What a way to send men back to their units! That evening as we waited for a ship to pick us up, Ervin pointed out a supply dump about 50 yards back up the beach with mountains of K rations and other supplies, which was guarded by four soldiers who kept walking around the supply dump in pairs. They took about fifteen minutes to make a complete round. They were armed with rifles. Should we take a chance and try to steal a few rations and possibly get shot by our own men? The enemy had shot at us for three weeks, so what's a little rifle fire from your own side?

About a half a dozen of us sneaked up to the supply dump just as soon as the guards walked by. In the half darkness the K ration boxes were brought to the edge of the dump, so the boxes could be carried away after the guards passed the next time around. While looking for more K rations I came upon a large box. I brought it to the edge of the dump. As soon as the guards passed around the corner of the supply dump, the boxes of rations were picked up and everyone made a quick dash for the shore. We had become instant heroes with the other troops who were watching the proceedings from their safe position on the beach.

Opening the K rations, cigarettes were the first thing taken out; the food was given away to whoever wanted to eat it, but the jackpot was hit with one of the boxes, as it was full of cartons of cigarettes.

We were awakened early in the morning from our bed of sand to be told to prepare to board a tramp steamer that had just arrived for our trip back to Sicily.

Once the troops had all been taken aboard, the ship left as silently as it had arrived in the half light of dawn. Everyone took to exploring the ship and trying to find a place to rest away from the main body of troops on the ship. As it grew light over the dark sea, one could see other ships rendezvousing and corvettes pulling alongside the ships as protection on the way back to Sicily.

As the morning broke into early afternoon, a lovely smell was coming from a porthole near where I was standing. Looking into the porthole a small mess hall came into view with sailors sitting and standing around tables bared to their midriffs eating pork chops. Taking my shirt and leggings off so as to look like a member of the crew, I went into the mess hall, making sure I didn't make the same mistakes when I was discovered in the Navy mess on the *Florence Nightingale*.

Walking in nonchalantly and picking up a tray, I walked over to where the chef was doling out the food. Into my tray went two luscious-looking pork chops, potatoes, and a piece of apple pie. Walking in a daze because of the prospect of eating this meal, I walked over to the furthest table from the members of the crew, fearing someone might recognize me as an outsider. Halfway through my meal I heard someone yell through the port hole, "What are you doing in there?" Looking up I saw Ervin. Raising my finger to my lips, signaling him to be quiet and to come in, I started to eat hurriedly, for I knew it wouldn't be long once the troops on the outside saw a few of us in here, the mess hall would be overflowing with Army personnel.

A sailor came over and sat down next to me and with a British accent claimed he had never seen me in the crew and asked if I was an American. Answering in the affirmative as I gulped on the remains of my second pork chop, he told me that this was a British merchant marine ship and they were British sailors carrying supplies to wherever needed in the Mediterranean Sea. As I started on my apple pie and coffee a yell came from where the chef was standing, "What are you soldiers doing here?" Looking up, a line of soldiers had come into the mess hall. From then on, I learned to keep a low profile wherever I went. Ervin had been served without being noticed, but the other soldiers had dashed in so fast and hadn't even removed their shirts—hardly a way to go without being pointed out as a soldier. Ervin had just seated himself when one of the kitchen help came over and tried to take his tray away; Ervin ran out holding one pork chop, with the second in his mouth, and the pie in his other hand. I followed him with the rest of the pie in my mouth, gulping the coffee left in my cup, and laughing and choking as I reached the outer deck of the ship. Once my mouth had cleared, I denounced the chefs and then the soldiers for not being more tactful so everyone could have walked into the mess hall quietly and been fed. To hell with it, why should I get involved with a bunch of guys I didn't even know?

Chapter Six

Palermo

The ship steamed through the quiet Mediterranean sea—what a contrast from the first time that I had been in a convoy that landed on that island.

After almost two days on the British merchant marine ship, it reached land and the soldiers disembarked and were trucked to a replacement depot, a place where soldiers were gathered together to be placed or returned to the unit that they had left.

Living in pup tents, it began to feel like the living conditions that had been endured by the soldiers who had invaded Sicily. The food was terrible, so a few or us thought it would be better to go into town to barter our cigarettes for whatever could be found. Walking down the street with our sleeves rolled, no ties, needing shaves; this certainly wasn't what a rear echelon soldier should look like, but being combat soldiers who gave a damn? Besides, what could be done with one so outrageously dressed? One could only be sent back to his combat unit.

As four of us strolled down the streets of Palermo, three officers passed wearing neckties, shoes shined, and looking like rear echelon disciplinarians. Having gone by these officers for a distance of 5 yards or so, a loud command was heard, "Halt you soldiers!" A major quickly caught up with us and asked why we looked like we did and why the officers hadn't been saluted. Here was a rear echelon bastard from

S4 who was enjoying the fruits of what the combat units had left him and his fellow officers to enjoy, and they were agitated because the proper respect hadn't been shown them.

The Major after dressing us down, demanded our names and unit, "I know your division, by your shoulder patch. What's your regiment and company?"

"George Winston, 180th regiment, I Company," I answered.

One of his lackeys took the information. Upon hearing my new name, the other fellows with me gave fictitious names. Walking away laughing, the major couldn't understand our joviality. The dummy, all he had to look down at our dog tags and he would have seen our real names, but I figured him right—a typical rear echelon boob.

Back to the repo depot where the news came over the radio that the British 8th Army had invaded Italy at the boot in Calabria, and I thought we probably would have an invasion around Rome where we would meet up with them.

Every day names were called out. The GIs were told that they were to be returned to their units. They were to get their belongings together and report back in an hour.

Three days after I reached the repo depot my name was called along with Ervin, who immediately told me not to answer it, as the sergeant calling my name didn't know me or him and we could stall going back to our unit and possibly combat. He said they would call us only once or twice and then call other names, and our names wouldn't come up again for a couple of weeks, as there were so many men in this camp. The sergeant called my name a half dozen times and then started on the next ones. My conscience started to get to me. Going over the hill in Tunis from the hospital was excusable, but refusing to go back to one's unit to avoid possible combat conditions was against my principles. After 15 minutes or so, I reported to the sergeant. He asked me if I had the GIs (upset stomach). That was my out. "Yes, I was at the latrine when you called my name." He asked if I was all right now. Smiling, I answered, "Yes," surely feeling a thousand times better because I erased a taint of evading my duty. It made my body feel if I had just had a soothing hot shower.

Getting into the truck, finding a seat, relaxing, thinking Ervin had decided to stay, but looking back to the tent where the CP was, Ervin was talking to the sergeant and pointing toward the truck. On he came, running, his conscience was no different from mine—a good soldier.

The truck bounced around for a couple of hours until we were left off at a sign that said 179th regiment. Ervin and I separated not to meet again until Anzio. A jeep took me to the 3rd battalion, but the place seemed deserted. Walking over to where a sign said Headquarters Company, no one was in sight. Sitting down to ponder the situation, a voice broke out "Syd!" Turning around, I came face to face with Felix Suvervi, who was the company clerk.

"Where is everybody?" I demanded. He told me that I had just missed the battalion. They had just moved out that morning and put on LSTs with the rest of the regiment. He was left behind to take care of the company's baggage.

"Each company left one man behind to take care of the baggage. If everything goes all right, the baggage will be loaded tomorrow and we'll be on the LST with it, so take it easy. You'll have to stay here until we load up to join the unit." Then he told me he was surprised to see me as he had heard that I was in an accident and hurt badly enough not to return to the outfit. He pulled out a few cans from a K ration box and said, "Let's eat."

The next day, over the radio came the news that Italy had surrendered. What did that mean? Could it be possible that the Germans would pull out of Italy? Never, I told Subvervi.

Then, on September 9 over the radio, came the news that Salerno had been invaded by a American army, the 5th Army under General Clark. Why General Clark? What the hell was the matter with Patton? We had good luck with the old bastard. Subvervi told me that the troops had been entertained by Bob Hope and he had put on a good show and that there wasn't much new with the company, except some captain from the first division had come up to see me while I was in the hospital. That had to be Norm Adelman, a fellow from my hometown, who I had gone to school with back in New London. The next day, September 10 we were alerted to be ready to more out with the baggage. A truck was sent up that afternoon and we started loading the baggage. After dropping off the baggage, an LST came back for us. and the rest of the battalion personnel. To my astonishment one of the men coming to us was an officer, a lieutenant from M Company, the same one back in Fort Devens who had called us "yellow Yankee bastards" and said that he would teach us how to fight.

"Subvervi," I said, "What hell is he doing here? How come he's not with M Company, where he belongs?"

"Any enlisted man can take care of the baggage," Subvervi said. "He must be scared shitless. If that was one of us, they would probably court-martial the hell out of us."

He wasn't the first to show bravado in noncombat situations and then turn to jelly in combat.

As I walked into the LST, a thought came to me: here was the third ship I had been on in the last three months. What a traveler—I even had an airplane ride! The LST laid over in port that night; it was just as well for the regiment was catching hell. The next day we rendezvoused with the 180 regiment and headed for Italy, passing what seemed to be the Isle of Capri, and that song, "It was on the Isle of Capri where I found her," came to mind.

Chapter Seven

Salerno

As we came to land, and debarked on a sandy beach, I learned this was Salerno. German planes were bombing anything in the water; destroyers were firing their guns directly over the beach. Confusion was everywhere. Who the hell ordered the baggage delivered in this hellhole? What the hell had happened to the regiment? Had they gone inland and let the Germans take over the beach? Guns of all kinds were going off. In the confusion, Subvervi and I got off with a truck that had our baggage and went a couple of miles up the road where everything was stalled. Tanks were milling around; shells were falling all over. Stuka dive bombers were dropping their bombs. Why the hell didn't I stay in that repo depot for a couple of more days?

Unloading the baggage from the truck, Subvervi and I settled down waiting for the artillery barrage to ease up, but the shells soon were interspersed with machine gun fire coming across the field. We were wondering what was coming next as we lay in a ditch by the side of the road; had we walked or driven into a German trap? Whose bright idea was it to land the baggage so close to D-Day? What had happened to the battalion? Were they free of the action on this beachhead? Were they catching as much hell as we were?

Leaving Subvervi and the baggage, I thought heading in a north-easterly direction would get me close to my regiment. Going into the 157th regimental area brought me no closer to my outfit. I found out that the 179th had been cut off and was going in another direction. After making contact with the rest of the division, I tried to make my way in the general direction of my regiment. Why the hell was I doing this with everything breaking loose all around us? But it was better than being back near that lousy Salerno Beach which seemed to be zeroed in on by every German 88 Stuka dive bomber and Messerschmidt the Nazis had in Italy. Someone in the 157th regimental pointed out the general direction of the 179th and told me to wait a day before starting out, and I did, though this regiment was drawing heavy fire. Getting a ride with a jeep that was going in the direction of my unit, I was off for better or worse.

The road down which we traveled was almost free of those devastating 88s. Could it be that those Nazi bastards had run out of ammunition, or were they withdrawing?

The jeep driver left me off at regimental headquarters where the general direction of my battalion was pointed out. It was a mile or so away—quite close quarters for a battalion headquarters to be so close to regimental headquarters. As I got closer, gazing at the OP, I immediately started looking for someone in my company. Sure enough it didn't take me long to find Sergeant Frisbee, who was so surprised to see me, he would have thrown a party for me if he could.

"I heard you were badly hurt in a truck accident; I never expected to see you come back. Why did you?"

I guess Frisbee had missed my bitching. Why else would he be glad to see someone who had ridiculed every officer and sergeant in the company? Frisbee asked me how come I had come back at this time; he always considered me smart. He actually had a tear in his eye, for he didn't think anyone would want to come back to a combat unit, especially with all the action going on. Of course, I still had a little green in me and combat still seemed to hold an aura of strength and challenged my intestinal fortitude. As we were talking the incoming artillery seemed to subside. Frisbee said it was the first time in a week that it had been so quiet. The first sergeant showed me around to the different platoons so I could say hello. Hook greeted me with a big smile, but one could easily see the whole platoon was shaken by the experiences of the past week. A few casualties had been removed, one of whom was Hogan, a likable Irishman from New York. As the casualties were added up, the price of war seemed to become more imbedded in my mind.

As Frisbee and I headed back to the company CP (command post), it seemed to be awfully quiet. We couldn't hear the clatter of the machine guns or the constant explosions of the incoming (artillery shells). Could it be that the enemy was pulling out? It was elements of another division going through our lines and going in the general direction of the enemy. Frisbee was so glad to see me; he kept me hanging around with him and the fellows who hung around the battalion CP. He told me he had gotten an official order from the colonel who was in charge of the hospital where I had been telling Frisbee to bring court-martial charges against me for taking off from the hospital for Tunis. He told me he tore up the order and called the colonel every name in the book. "That rear echelon son of a bitch wanting to court-martial you; that's a hell of a nerve."

The battalion laid around for a few days and then moved northeastward toward the center of Italy. Then we rode in Frisbee's jeep and behind the line companies. We were in clear view of the German tanks on the hills above us, and 88s were constantly being thrown down on the advancing troops. Jumping out of the jeep at the first sound of a whistle became a nuisance, but it was pure folly to sit in the jeep as the shells were striking close by. It came to a point where I started walking rather than riding in the jeep. It was closer to the ditches along the roadside.

As the convoy crawled along, I could look back and see the trucks of the other companies. Riding on the baggage of one truck was the lieutenant who had berated all the northerners as yellow bastards back at Ft. Deven; I wondered how his feelings were? Would he be court-martialed? What would have happened to him if he didn't come from Oklahoma? To hell with worrying about him. I had to give Frisbee an answer as to what unit I wanted to go back in—intelligence, A&P or the kitchen. Frisbee had given me an out. The kitchen was where I would be less likely to get hit with enemy fire. I felt insulted when he mentioned the kitchen—me a kitchen helper; how dare he? I might not be much of a combat soldier, but certainly mot a mess hall attendant. Yet I should have realized he was doing me a favor; there were plenty of guys who would have given anything for such an opportunity. Let me think it over, I told Frisbee, and that was the way it stood for the next few weeks as we traveled through the mountains of central Italy.

The intelligence section to which I had been first attached in Sicily seemed to have been fragmented. The section sergeant had been evacuated after Salerno. Delano told me the section sergeant had been ordered to go up a hill to set up an OP by the battalion colonel and had refused. He was threatened with a court-martial by the battalion colonel. What happened after that was never made clear, but he was evacuated with many others—some for wounds, and others for psychological reasons. Corporal Schultz, the other noncom besides me was put in charge, but the men were everywhere and there seemed to be much disorganization in my former section. Delano had set up the OP when the sergeant chickened out, but never got the recognition for this feat, a situation where enemy fire continually fell on the hill until there was more steel than grass on the hill.

It was in this climate that our company moved along through central Italy where it was more mountainous than hilly. Thus, we reached the outskirts of Benevento around the end of September.

The column was halted and immediately the men on either side of the road went into the fields that lay alongside the road. It would be suicide to just lay along the roadside, where one could be an easy target for strafing by enemy planes or get torn to pieces from shrapnel exploding along the roadside from tanks stationed on the hills above the road the troops were moving on. While laying about 25 yards off the road in a ravine, someone yelled out my name. "Syd, come take a look at these troops." Getting up warily, I walked slowly toward the road, wondering what sights would befall my eyes. Looking straight at the road in disbelief, there were soldiers slowly making their way along the roadside in two columns, but what was so different about these men? They were Japanese dressed in American uniforms. Someone commented that Japan had surrendered and decided to join the Allies against the Germans. As we watched this column of soldiers move through our positions, one could see the 100th battalion insignia on their shirtsleeves. We were really watching Americans of Japanese ancestry walk by; they had been put into one unit and segregated from the rest of the U.S. Army. What we didn't know at the time was that this 100th Battalion made up of Japanese Americans would become the most decorated and one of the best combat units in the U.S. Army. This unit was continually used as a point to assault the enemy and whenever the 100th battalion was brought into action, one knew it would be used to break through the enemy lines. It later was broadened to become a regiment, the 442nd, and I had the honor of meeting a few of the men from this unit on Anzio.

So as the 100th battalion passed quietly by, the men of our outfit watched in amazement. A new element had been brought into the minds of the men, but there were no derogatory remarks made about the ancestry of these men, for battle is a great equalizer and no man dare risk deriding another man, for during battle he might be the first to break, and if one has a conscience, the humiliation could become unbearable.

Moving through Benevento, our battalion was constantly harassed by German tanks on the hills that always seemed to be in front of us as we walked along through the roads and fields.

It was along one of these hilly roads that seemed to be made up entirely of curves that we came upon some of our tanks tied down by enemy artillery fire. They were firing back, but this was no place for an unprotected infantry man. But where could we run as the shrapnel bounced off the tanks and into the ditches where we had taken refuge? Laying there quietly waiting for the shelling to stop, a voice came booming out of one of the tanks! It was a radio announcer coming over American Radio Services describing the World Series from the States. Since, I had no place to go and wouldn't have tried to go even if I could, I lay there and listened to the World Series of 1943 in a most unusual position. At times it was difficult to hear the announcer's voice above the sound of the incoming 88s.

When the shells eased off, the radio in the tank could be heard for quite a distance. Most likely the enemy even got a taste of American baseball on that hilly Italian road.

Moving along through the mountainous roads, the troops came to the outskirts of Piedmonte D'Alife, but before we got close to that town, my contact with a German weapon new to me came with great surprise. It was nicknamed the Screaming Memies. This was really an artillery piece that had six barrels and fired six mortar shells at the same time. It left a weird screaming noise to fill one's ears. If one hadn't moved one's bowels up to that time, they were sure to be moved—that was guaranteed. The attack had stalled and some of us in the rear were called up to the forward battalion CP, which was situated in an old stone farmhouse with the line companies surrounding the area. As we moved through the artillery fire riding in a jeep, it turned over going around a curve. Did I get hurt falling out? Of course not, my luck hadn't changed. Making my way on foot to the CP, I noticed ambulances being loaded with wounded GIs. Going inside the stone farmhouse, ten or so soldiers were huddled around a fireplace cooking up coffee in their cups. One of the soldiers told me he had had enough for the day and nonchalantly told me his brother had been wounded earlier in the day. After they had placed him in an ambulance and the vehicle started to take off, it received a direct hit from an enemy artillery shell, killing everyone in the ambulance. Telling him I was sorry, while walking slowly away, I ran right into my company commander.

The captain grabbed me by the arm and yelled out, "Schultz, I've got a good man for you! Looking in amazement at the captain, I didn't dare ask what he meant, but knowing him the future didn't look too bright for me. The captain told me to go along with Schultz on a patrol to a hill just overlooking our positions and try to see what the Germans were doing on the other side. Why did I, I thought, not even being with intelligence any more, have to go into that farm house? Why couldn't I learn to stay put in the cold and rain where officers were as scarce as hot food. Up the hill our two-man patrol went, moving very cautiously, sometimes not moving at all, finally making the top of the hill and moving easily from one tree to another until a position overlooking the valley where the Germans were encamped came into view. There they were down there moving around as if they were back home. There was no unusual activity; whereas, they should be getting ready to move out since we were breathing down their asses. They were probably as tired as the troops who were chasing them, or they had decided to make a stand. Just then a few mortar shells dropped almost in front of us as we lay looking through our field glasses from the deepest ravine that could be found at the top of the hill.

"I think it's time to get the hell out of here," Schultz yelled out, and I was out of my cover before his last word was uttered. We made our way out of the wooded area in double time as the mortars started to really zero in on the position that we had held a few seconds earlier.

The Germans raked the crest of the hill with artillery fire every half hour or so, just in case the enemy might be up there. This was a normal procedure in war, done by both sides when high ground overlooks one side's position. We had been lucky. Inside that half hour, we had gone to the crest of the hill and were starting on the way back before the enemy artillery started to fall heavily. Moving swiftly, we were at the base of the hill before it was raked with 88s to Screaming Memies. Just in time!

After coming down from the hill and reporting into the battalion CP, Schultz and I walked over to where Frisbee was standing and he told the first sergeant that he couldn't take it anymore. Who could?

Whereas, the first sergeant told him he could be part of the kitchen help. This he accepted. Looking at me Frisbee said, "Well?" to which my response was a quick turn on my heel and I walked away. What a dunce! My last chance to get into the kitchen and I snubbed the opportunity. I would live to regret it.

The battalion colonel had been relieved, not for making any mistakes but because he refused to continue after the enemy immediately as division had demanded. Colonel Taylor wanted to give his men a little rest for a few hours, but the guys in command in the rear wouldn't hear of it, and relieved him of command.

On we moved through central Italy toward the Volturno River. Moving across the countryside by foot was the safest way to go; one could always try to dive into the closest ditch or ravine at the sound of a whistle of an artillery shell or of a strafing enemy plane. Crossing a field and reaching the top of a hill, the company was halted and we lay below the crest, smoking, when the sound of planes came out of the sky, right above us. No more than 10 yards up, a dozen Messerschmidts came roaring; the planes were flying low in order to avoid our antiaircraft on the way back to their base. The whole company had been caught flat-footed laying alongside the hill. Why the enemy planes hadn't strafed us was a mystery! Maybe they were out of ammunition or they were as surprised to see us as we were to see them. What a lucky break! I thought we were done for; in fact, if I had reached up, my hand could have touched one of the wheels of a plane.

Right after the planes went over, a battery of 105 artillery pieces pulled up in the ravine below us and started firing shells at the enemy on the other side of the hill. Looking over the top of the hill, the enemy could be seen retreating at a fast pace as our artillery shells started to catch up with their line of retreat.

Moving along, the battalion came to the Volturno River. Two line companies from another battalion had already crossed it earlier in the day under heavy fire and as we looked at the river, there was a pontoon bridge going up; it was being built by men of the 120th Engineer's Battalion. There they were working in full view of the

German artillery observers and braving the enemy fire. What guts, I thought.

It started to rain as we waited for the signal to cross the bridge. How much more miserable could it get—soaked to the skin, getting shot at, and being out of cigarettes—yet I could be one of those engineers out there building the bridge. Maybe I was lucky after all.

As I lay there, my mind reverted to the area we had just passed through. Who could blame the hundreds of Italians trudging down the road away from the combat areas to positions far in the rear? At times a bit of jealousy rose in my mind. Of these civilians moving away from this hell on earth, sometimes I wished that I was one of them.

Awakened from my dreams by a loud voice shouting. "Let's go," our company started moving across the bridge in trucks, which made it even more dangerous as the enemy shells were whistling around the bridge in a constant downpour. It was a relief to get to the other side and detruck. Then the unit started moving through the olive trees that dotted the landscape. A few dead soldiers lay alongside the trees, some covered by blankets and others in the same position as when they were hit by earlier enemy fire. The enemy seemed to have an inexhaustible supply of artillery shells for they kept up a constant barrage. Why more of us didn't get a sliver of shrapnel in our posterior remains a mystery? Continuing to move through the olive trees, the company finally reached the higher ground on the other side and instead of going down the road to the town, the troops headed for the higher. For a moment, I thought we were going to climb the side of the mountains that bordered on our left, but just then some troops could be seen picking their way up the mountain pass. Looking through my field glasses, I saw the insignia on their sleeves. They were men from the 82nd Airborne. They were being sent up the mountainside to protect our left flank from enemy sniper or machine gun fire.

Reaching the high ground, one could look back and see the flat land of the valley and the Volturno River. How easy it was for an enemy observer to train artillery fire down on the advancing troops.

The next day as I awoke and looked down from this elevated position, much of our own artillery units had filled the valley below. How quickly they had crossed the river and filled the valley with their guns, which were covered with their camouflaged nettings. There came a noise from the sky as if a thousand trucks were all trying to go up an icy grade in the middle of winter. As I looked up, the morning sky was filled with American bombers. In fact, they almost made it look as if a gigantic cloud was passing under the sun. Poking Hook in the ribs as we lay alongside the crest of the hill, I yelled out in delight, "Those Nazi bastards are going to get it now." But my smile soon left my face when to my amazement bombs started dropping on our artillery in the valley below us. Was I dreaming? Maybe my vision was getting bad. What the hell is going on? There goes some more planes dropping bombs. Can't these idiots see the guns pointing in a northerly direction? Our planes had come from the south. With an Air Corps like that who needs enemies? The poor artillery men—it was bad enough to get enemy planes strafing and bombing your positions, but when your own planes drop their bombs on their own artillery, what do you do? Do you open up with your antiaircraft guns? It was the fault of the lead plane, which is supposed to find the enemy positions and then drop its load of bombs. If the Air Corps bombs their own side in broad daylight, how can anyone believe all their supposedly successful bombing raids that are reported to the public. It's a good thing the pilots of the planes were in a hurry to drop their bombs and get out of there because there weren't many hits.

After this exhilarating experience, the company was alerted to move out and the battalion moved to take Venufro, which was taken early in the afternoon. Then as everyone looked around at the mountains and wondered what was next, Sergeant Rerter came over to me and said that I was due to go on a five-day pass to Naples. The division had initiated five-day furloughs for men on the line; three men were to go from my company. My name had been picked, as it was next in line for a furlough before we left the States.

"When do I leave?" was my excited question.

"First thing in the morning, you'll catch a jeep to regimental, where you'll be trucked back to Naples," Sergeant Rerter answered.

Chapter Eight

Naples

Awakened the next morning by a few incoming artillery shells and the voices of the other two men who were also going on furlough, I quickly got out of the muddy ditch that had been my lodging for the night and ran with the other men to the jeep that was to carry us away from this nightmare.

After getting to regimental, the men were directed to the trucks that were to take us to our first vacations on Italian soil. As the truck made its way back over the pontoon bridge that hung over the Volturno River, I kept wondering if the enemy was still dropping artillery shells around the site of the bridge. My wonderment didn't have to wait too long. A few shells were still being fired in the general direction of the bridge, but nothing like the ferocity when my first crossing was made. As the truck reached the other side and was off the bridge and made a turn in the road, a sigh of relief could be heard coming from every seat on the truck.

Arriving in Naples, the men were left out in front of a building that was situated on a hilly section right by the Bay of Naples. Ships of all kinds were anchored in the harbor; balloons stretched out over the ships as protection from low-flying German fighter and bombing planes. The building had been an old fort or something of the kind and was being used as a vacation spot for all the men from the combat units on their five day furloughs.

The first thing upon entering the building, everyone was told to disrobe and take a shower. The hot water felt real good and the men were given fresh clothing. Of course that was a problem for me as I couldn't wear the wool clothing that was handed out. My old clothes were practically in tatters, even if they had been washed and handed back, so I went around in a dry towel for a while trying to make a lieutenant in command understand that my difficulty with the clean uniforms was that I was allergic to wool. He asked me what the hell I was doing in the army if I needed special clothes? I was thinking he was making fun of me when he probably knew that my allergy could have gotten me out of the service. I told him he'd better get me a soft officer's shirt and pants. Telling me to sit down for a few minutes and have a smoke, he went rushing out of the shower area. About fifteen minutes later, he came back carrying the clothes I wanted. He smiled at me and said, "Have a good time in Naples, soldier; you can sleep and eat here for the five nights you're in Napoli or go out on your own, but be back here in five days to get your transportation back to your unit."

Setting off with the other two men who had come from my company, we walked into the center of Naples. People were rushing all over the streets; rear echelon soldiers filled the roads as they passed the young girls in the streets that propositioned every GI that passed by. The excitement of a big city in wartime was a unique experience to me. Cellars had become nightclubs; music emanated from the open doors and cellar windows. Before one could get close to the openings, one would be besieged by nine- or ten-year-old boys grabbing one's arms and yelling, "My sister sixteen. You want beef steak, Joe?" I was astounded. Where the hell did these little shits come from? They seemed to be doing a pretty good business with the newly arrived GIs. Later I heard from some of the GIs back in our sleeping quarters that the boys' sisters were really their grandmothers—not sixteen, but four times sixteen.

Going into one of the cellar nightclubs, it was comforting to sit down and listen to a few American songs played by Italian musicians and drink the cherry brandy which wasn't bad, though the price was exorbitant.

The first night I found my way back to my quarters even though the cherry brandy I'd consumed had me floating on air. I dropped on my cot, which to me at that time was more elegant and comfortable than any boudoir that Marie Antoinette ever graced with her charms. I don't know how long I had been sleeping before the whistling sound of bombs reached my ears, which weren't intoxicated like the rest of me. Waking from my sleep, sobriety quickly overcame me, for there's nothing like a few bombs to sober you up. It's a good formula when coffee won't do the trick. What the hell was going on? This was supposed to be a rest area. There was only one thought in my mind, and that was to get the hell out of there. Rushing over to some of the men looking out the window, I asked, "What the hell is going on?"

"They're trying to bomb the ships in the harbor. Those German bastards bomb almost every night," answered one of the men.

The ships in the harbor were the target but the bombs were coming awfully close to this old fort and it shook every time a bomb hit the nearby land. Well, I'm not sleeping here another night. I came here for a rest, not to get psycho, so the next day three of us left our lodgings at the fort and went over to the other side of town where we rented a room far away from the waterfront.

Going over to the Red Cross building, or to where the local U.S.O. building was located, it was full of rear echelon GIs. They seemed to monopolize everything in Naples, from the new combat boots to the new combat jackets, which were meant to be distributed to the men on the line first. But here in Naples these new styles were being modeled by every rear echelon soldier in sight, and that was the only way one was able to tell who the combat soldiers were, for they still wore their leggings. Their shoulder patches were nowhere to be seen because new outfits had been issued to everyone after their shower and none of the shirts had any unit insignia.

On the third day in Naples, the three of us were sitting in a nightclub cellar when a soldier walked in and started boasting to another soldier that he had just come back from the front and acted as it he had just defeated the enemy. Asking him what outfit he was with, he said his unit was a truck outfit that brought ammunition up to a division ammunition dump and that he got so close to the front that he could see the flashes of our artillery. When we heard that, he was almost laughed out of the place. His furthest penetration of the combat line was no more than 20 miles beyond the line. He was surprised to find out that we had just come from combat and I'm sure he was more careful when he went around boasting again because he found himself dumped in the roadside outside of the nightclub.

The Via Roma seemed like it was full of 10-year-old pimps, and rear echelon soldiers selling anything from cigarettes to clothing on the black market. War made prostitutes of all descriptions. Still it was a more viable and happy scene than the area we had just come from, which was drab and had an aura of death.

Five days went by quickly and the trucks were waiting to take us back to our units. As the trucks went up the hills that surrounded Naples, a question came to mind; would I ever get back to this city?

Chapter Nine

Back to Combat: Italy

It started to rain again as soon as the trucks left Naples, but at least we were protected by the canvas covering of the trucks. In fact, there hadn't been much sunshine during the month of October and now it was almost the middle of November.

Getting back to the unit, everyone wanted to know if I had a good time and what was it like back there. Those who were going next asked what to look out for, so my warning about sleeping in that old fort that was bombed almost every night was taken with enthusiasm.

Venafro had been taken and our company was situated on a hill outside of town where the narrow road curved its way between the hills up to the mountains. The Germans commanded the hill on the other side of the road. Our job was to guard the forward battalion CP. At first, some took over the slit trenches that the Germans had dug when they occupied this hill, but one had to do it warily in case these foxholes had been booby-trapped, a favorite trick of the Germans. The rain continued with everyone soaked through, but no one could even catch a good cold when it was needed badly. The Germans were no better off, for the next day while the rain was coming down, as I was observing a house on the hill opposite us, about forty or so German soldiers got out of their holes and ran for the lone house. Why did they do it so openly? They must have really been soaked to the skin. Probably they spent their nights there. Whatever the reason an artillery barrage was called in on the house. Once the shells started exploding around the house, a white flag appeared from the doorway. The artillery was called off and the Germans stepped out to surrender to a patrol sent out to pick them up. As we watched them pick their way down the side of the hill, one of the German soldiers stepped on a mine that had been laid by their own men. Our patrol made the Germans march in front of them; if anyone was to step on one of their mines, it would be their own men. Watching the Germans pick up their own man who had wandered into their minefield was ironic as those mines were laid down to entrap the American troops.

As the captured Germans made their way into our lines carrying their wounded comrades, my attention went back to the soaking rain that seemed to be filling the foxhole in which I now was standing. However, the rain had other benefits. The enemy seemed to have stopped firing artillery shells for a while. Standing like this, soaked, one wondered why pneumonia or at the least a cold wouldn't be in the offing for one out in these elements. No such luck, though. One couldn't even catch a cold if one was in a combat unit.

The next day, the first sergeant came up to see how things were. He told me that the German soldier who had stepped on the mine had his leg amputated by the battalion aid doctor. The soldier didn't know why the doctor had to amputate his leg, so he asked the doctor who told him gangrene was spreading and that was the only way he could stop it. He said at first he was a little suspicious because the doctor was Jewish and he just took off the German's leg for spite, but that his suspicions were for naught and he was sorry to have had such thoughts.

Then he went on to tell me that he had just heard that Lieutenant Russo had been killed in the Salerno area. What a shame! He was one officer I had gotten along with. The Okies had gotten him transferred out of the unit. He was the type of guy that would charge a machine gun single-handedly.

The next day about a dozen of us were called down from our

positions on the hill to a stone house on the bottom of the hill where we met up with the platoon lieutenant and were told to follow his jeep up the road for about a half mile where supplies that were laying in the trailer attached to the jeep were to be carried up the side of the steep hills to the line companies. As there was no way to reach them by road, it was to be packed on mules. However, there were no mules available at this time, so we were pressed into carrying the supplies to the line companies on our backs.

We went up the road until we got to the base of this semi-mountain; then the supplies were unloaded just as we were spotted by the enemy. Shells started falling all over the place. The lieutenant who was supposed to lead us to the line companies told his driver to take off back to our lines just as soon as the jeep was unloaded. The son of a bitch; what a leader!

Then the supplies were picked up and we started carrying them under the most adverse conditions; for example, as the shells came down on us like a rainstorm. Halfway up the hill, the men stopped to rest when two scouts from I Company came down upon us. After telling us where their company was located they took off down the hill and up the hill on the other side as we watched. About halfway up the other side they were suddenly encompassed by small explosions. As we watched, the Germans boxed them in with mortar fire. The poor bastards had walked into full view of a German observation post and were being blasted with mortars. Ten minutes later the shelling stopped, but those two soldiers we had talked to only a little while earlier didn't move. Who was going to go over to the other hill to see if they were still alive? Just then a patrol came down from the crest of the hill and gave us a hand carrying the supplies to their company.

Leaving I Company and coming back down the hill to the narrow road where we had left the jeep, we waited for the lieutenant to come back as he had yelled he would earlier. After waiting for about a half hour, we started to walk down the road warily as it had been under shell fire all afternoon.

Just as we approached this complex of a church and two or three buildings, all hell broke loose. As it was starting to get dark, we ran for the first building that was handy. It was the church and it was already full of civilians and GIs. Everyone sat quietly in the half darkness while artillery shells exploded off the outer walls of the church making almost everyone cringe with fear. People were sobbing all over the place; small children were crying in fear and to my surprise one of the soldiers in my squad was sobbing as loud as the civilians. I offered him a cigarette, hoping his tears would dry and he would not embarrass us, but he continued weeping forcing me to move away from him.

The barrage lasted about an hour; it was completely dark when the shelling stopped, but no one moved. This place seemed as safe as any, and the rain didn't penetrate the roof of the church. Someone opened the church door and yelled for any GIs inside to come out as everyone was wanted in a hurry. As I sat there I deliberated whether to go or continue to sit there for the rest of the night, as no one knew who was who in the darkened church. The first sergeant put his head in the door and yelled for any GIs to come out, for it was an emergency. Finally deciding to move, I went outside where half the company was loading K rations and ammunition on their backs to bring to the line companies up on the hills. Quickly joining the rest of the men, my back was loaded like a mule's and the men headed up the road that we had traveled earlier in the day to bring supplies to the men in the hills. Halfway up the road shells starting falling on this small village. For some reason the men on the road weren't shelled; this raised a question in my mind. The soldiers were the logical target; the enemy must have spotted our column but the shells went over our heads straight for the church and the other buildings in the area. As the troops started to climb the hill, a flash could be seen on the other hillside. It was an artillery piece being fired; somehow the Germans had hidden it on the side of the hill and it was zeroed on the village. They weren't able to fire on us because if it was moved it would have fallen right off of this semi-cliff; counter battery fire was called for and this seemed to quiet the enemy artillery piece.

Having completed our task, everyone made their way warily back to the area of the church when an immense enemy barrage started. Running in all directions, looking for cover in the dark was enough to make one a candidate for the nuthouse. Spotting a ditch by the roadside, it didn't take long to jump in and hit the bottom of the ditch at the speed my legs were going. While laying there a yell came from a few yards up the road. The lieutenant had come running down the road like everyone else and when he jumped into the ditch, there was someone already lying there. He came down full force on a soldier named Cavallo, almost breaking his back. A shell exploded alongside the ditch. The lieutenant lost a couple of fingers. We were told he was given first aid and evacuated by the medics, never to come back. How lucky could one get?

The next day, the first Battalion went through our position and Neil Shea stopped to say hello in one of the buildings we had quartered ourselves in that day. After comparing notes about home for a few minutes, he moved on with his company. Our company was able to relax that day, and as it we hadn't had enough excitement the past week, Corporal Raly decided to have a little fun. Unknown to us he had emptied the powder from a hand grenade and fixed the area where the firing pin was situated, so when he pulled the firing pin the grenade wouldn't go off. However, he did it wrong, so when he pulled the firing pin in a room where about ten of us were sitting, everyone ran out. A good thing because the grenade went off and splattered in all directions. No one got hurt, but Corporal Raly was very apologetic. He realized his horsing around could have killed some of his own men.

A few shells fell in the area of the building we slept in that night, but none hit the building. Waking up the next morning, Corporal Hook called me out to take a look at an unexploded 88 artillery shell laying right outside the door. What luck that it hadn't exploded.

An order came down from regiment that hot food was to be served to the men whenever possible, so the kitchens were moved up as close as possible to their companies. Our kitchen moved past us in

Polizzi into the hills at Filignano, a sort of village dug into the side of the hill and as we rode or walked up the road we could see on the hill on the right an 88 artillery piece dug into the side of the mountain; it had perfect camouflage. It only fired at night. The enemy didn't man it during the day for fear of being observed. This gun was zeroed right at the village of Polizzi. That's why they had been so accurate with their fire. To think General Clark had gone up that road only a week or so earlier to get a first-hand look at the front line. It was funny how his jeep had come around a curve in the road to a point where we could look down on him from our foxholes on the hill. His driver had yelled out asking the way to I Company. We thought we were getting nutty when we saw the jeep contained a three-star general. We told him it wasn't safe to go any further in the jeep. The general didn't listen and told his driver to continue up the road. Watching them depart in a cloud of dust toward the hill that contained I Company and the enemy, we waited for the enemy artillery to start. Miraculously it didn't. A half hour later the noise of a jeep could be heard racing down the road. Then around the curve came General Clark and his driver. Not stopping, they continued back to the rear. About five minutes later enemy artillery opened up, raking the entire roadway. They had spotted the dust on the road but took their time firing their artillery. If they had known it was General Clark we would have been in for a real heavy barrage. Generals weren't only to be found in the rear; every once in a while a general would come up to where the action was to see for himself how desperate the situation might be for his troops in the field.

The job of my platoon became bringing ammunition up to the line companies so our main headquarters became the town of Polizzi and the jeep carried the supplies from there. The men would take turns accompanying the supplies in the jeeps as far as feasible and then with help from patrols from the line companies would carry them on foot to their destination.

It was during this time that Sergeant Rerter started riding the jeep to the line companies. For someone who was on the verge of being psycho he was showing unusual bravery. The fact that Platoon Lieutenant Rand had been evacuated after being wounded left the platoon without an officer. It then occurred to me that Sergeant Rerter was trying for a battlefield promotion. He wanted to become an officer. Every night he would ride the jeep up to the forward CP. As far as I was concerned, I only went when my turn came up; the other platoon noncoms didn't seem too anxious to move any more than I and I was still a buck private. Even the kitchen had been ordered to move up to the village of Filignano, where it was quartered in the cellar of a brick house and this was where Sergeant Harris, our mess sergeant, was killed. The poor guy was really a hell of a nice guy, and always showed me the greatest respect, even when I was busted to a private. So even kitchen personnel weren't safe in our outfit; it probably was a good thing that I turned down Sergeant Frisbee's offer to work in the kitchen, as two more men were killed who belonged to the kitchen personnel.

Replacements had come into the company to fill up the holes left by those who had been wounded, killed, or just got sick. Ira Fishman, Mike Kamenuck, and a few others had been evacuated to the hospital. Yellow jaundice seemed to be the sickness that could get one out of combat and to the rear hospital area, but how could one get lucky and catch yellow jaundice? Pneumonia was out, as my clothes had been soaked for a week from the continuous rains and the only thing I got from the wet weather was wet feet. Before Mike Kamenuck was evacuated, he told me how he had operated a movie camera for a movie news crew that had refused to get out of their hole. What a war! After Filignano had been captured and rid of Germans, a newsreel crew came into the town and asked us to recreate the taking of the town so they could put it on film and fool the people back hone into thinking they were watching the American soldiers. Cleaning out German snipers in the town—what a laugh. How many more of these farcical episodes were perpetrated on those back home who thought they were watching the real McCoy?

It was now well into December as the battalion reached for its last objective—the town of Lagone. New replacements were starting to fill up the empty spots our company had developed. One such replacement was a Japanese-American soldier named Toy. He was the only one of that background in the regiment, and at first everyone wondered why he hadn't been assigned to the 100th Battalion, the all Japanese-American outfit. He seemed to be embarrassed and kept his head down. I surmised he must have taken abuse in the rear areas, where the soldiers are well known for their bravado when it comes to doing anything with their mouths. He soon started walking around with his head up high as front line soldiers don't have time to deride someone because of his religious or racial background and it's only those who have just arrived from a rear area that usually start any trouble until they learn otherwise. It was just such a son of a bitch who made a remark about not wanting to hear about my Jewish views. That incident occurred in a house where Delano's section was relaxing. I hadn't run into anything like that before, so I grabbed this new recruit by the hair. He stood a good four or five inches taller than me and I started to throw him out of doors until Delano came over and told me the guy didn't know what he was saying and didn't mean it. I was going to kill the bastard. I didn't go through this kind of shit to have to listen to some prejudiced bastard come up from the rear. Never again did he come near me after he apologized. He left the outfit a long time before the war was over. That was one of the few incidents of anti-Semitism that I had bumped into while in the army. Whether remarks were made behind my back, I don't know. However, combat seems to rule out all forms of bigotry except by those making their first try at it. Toy was assigned to the kitchen and he ended up becoming the mess sergeant in Germany.

After Lagone was taken, the 180th regiment went through our positions to relieve our regiment. While laying by the side of the road, Filosi, whose brother was a machine gunner with the 180th Regiment, saw some men of his brother's company walk by. Asking where his brother was, they quietly told him he had been killed a few weeks back north of Venufro. Filosi's face fell. Poor Louis Filosi. He had been hardened to death, but this was family. Offering my condolences, he answered, "Wait until the family hears this back home."

It was almost Christmas and we had been relieved from action. Some forces of the Free French went through the town. They were Black Africans from Morocco called Goums. Mules, sheep, and some kind of whiskey were part of their belongings. We traded off what rations and cigarettes were available to us for their alcohol. That night part of our outfit was housed in that area and got ready for a Christmas party. It was where the forward CP had been located and I bumped into Frank Backus there. He was already half in the bag and it didn't take me long to catch up to him as we drank and drank and sang and sang into early Christmas morning as snow fluttered down outside the stone house.

It is hard to say what time the festivities ended, but there is one sure thing: it didn't get quiet in that place until all the whiskey was gone.

Waking up the next day by the yelling of some soldiers to come and get hot dough-nuts and coffee. It was well into the afternoon as I walked from the cellar to the first floor of the partly destroyed stone house. Outside, there was a Red Cross truck with about four Red Cross girls standing by a table that was holding pans of doughnuts and a coffeemaker from which the girls were pouring hot coffee to the officers of the battalion headquarters. Walking out with our own cups which still had the smell of whiskey emanating from the bottom, I pushed the cup into the waiting arm of one of the Red Cross girls while another handed out a few doughnuts to my other hand. The fact that the girls weren't too good-looking didn't deter anyone from being startled to see them up so close to where the action had been only a few days earlier.

As usual when any guests of the female gender came around to the battalion, it was the officers who acted as if they hadn't seen a woman for years, no matter how homely the girls might have been.

Later I asked John Left why he was bringing coffee and flour over to the Red Cross girls. He told me that they didn't come with their own supplies. When they would come to an area they would give a chit to the mess sergeant for the amount of coffee and flour and sugar they requisitioned from the army and the Red Cross was supposed to pay the government back, especially with all the money they collected from all the saps back home. John told me it never happened because regiment never collected the chits that he knew of. What a farce! The only thing the Red Cross provided was the doughnut machine and some homely girls for the officers to ogle. Better they never came. Our new mess sergeant was a baker by trade and when he got a chance he made some of the best doughnuts we could wish for. So as our regiment was pulled from the mountains northeast of Cassino, it was with a happy thought that combat conditions would be avoided for a while as the division was headed for a rest—possibly a hot shower, hot food, and just to be left alone. As I got into a vehicle to be carried down this tortuous road all thoughts of combat were receding from my mind. It was eighteen months since the regiment had left the states. Certainly one thing that had been lost was how to live like a human being. One became grateful for the least little thing; for example, such as to be out of the line of fire of the enemy. Anything else was a luxury.

CHAPTER TEN

Out of Range

The division went back across the Volturno River to a place out of range of all enemy fire except Hitler's airplanes. Tents had been set up, blankets had been distributed, and my barracks bag was waiting—and with it a fresh change of clothes after six weeks.

In this camp, everyone relaxed. Up on the hill was a house that looked a like a castle; it was occupied by an Italian who we were informed was a count and probably a Fascist bastard. Every day he would come down to hold a conversation with some of the men, asking such questions as where we were going next. Why he wasn't picked up was beyond me. He probably supplied girls to some of the regimental officers. Whenever he came into view the men would address him as "cunt," not "count" with everyone within earshot laughing.

A bulletin board had been set up outside the company CP with all the events listed on it that the soldiers could take part in. In the evening we listened to the BBC news. We had to listen to London to find out what was happening 50 miles north of our position.

On the bulletin board was a notice that Joe Brown was putting on a U.S.O. show the following afternoon at an amphitheater about 20 miles south of the camp. Hitching a ride from one of the numerous trucks moving along the road, I arrived well in advance of the performance. Walking down through the amphitheater, a sudden sense of foreboding came to me. What if there should be an enemy air raid; how the hell would one get out of this place in a hurry? Looking around at those occupying the front rows, they were mostly enlisted men. Officers usually took the best seats at every theatrical performance I had attended in the States. Why should it change here? The officers were probably thinking the same way as me and those enlisted men in the front seats were probably rear echelon men who had never sustained an air raid. Placing myself about halfway down in the amphitheater and near an exit, I lit up a cigarette and proceeded to relax in the still almost-empty amphitheater. Within a half hour, the place had filled up and Joe Brown came onstage and gave a stellar performance. It was well worth the trip, except that I felt awfully uneasy sitting there as my head was always turning skyward, looking, looking, and looking for any enemy planes.

The next few weeks were spent looking around, seeing men in the other companies whom I hadn't seen since Salerno, or going down to talk to the runners from the line companies. These men, two to A Company, were used to bring messages back and forth between company commanders and the battalion commander. Their usefulness becomes apparent when other means of communications are cut off. These men had to make contact with battalion under the most trying conditions—artillery barrages, machine gun fire, and minefields. They were a little more intelligent than the usual run-of-the-mill soldiers, so I enjoyed many a conversation with them. Most of them later were killed at Anzio. One such runner who became extremely friendly was a soldier named Jim Barry, a likable Irishman from the Boston area. He was extremely intelligent and one hell of a nice guy; our conversations would run well into the night. He was attached to M Company, a company I had started out with in the States. He was killed at Anzio, not more than 10 yards from where I was digging myself in with my fingernails.

On the bulletin board came another announcement of a U.S.O. show that had as its star attraction Humphrey Bogart with his wife

May Methot. In addition to this, his latest movie was to be shown outdoors on a screen that was to be set up on the stage where the live performances were to take place. It was about a tank battle in the desert between the Germans and Americans. Most of the fellows went to this show; it was held just at it got dark and just for the division. The stage was set in a hollow with the ground surrounding it sloping into small hills, thus making the area a perfect outdoor theater. There were no seats, but the soft grass made it comfortable to sit and even though it was January, the weather seemed to be extremely mild in this part of Italy north of Naples and south of Cassino.

It was a star-filled night and the only artificial light came from the spotlight shining down on the stage where Bogart and his wife appeared to a tumultuous cheer and hand clapping that sounded more like thunder coming down from the mountains. Mr. Bogart went on to kid the assembled soldiers by telling them he wanted them all to join his gang when the war was over, as they were pretty expert with firearms. Of course, Humphrey Bogart had become famous for his portrayals of gangsters in the movies. Quite a rapport developed between the movie star and his audience. After about a half hour of this type of conversation which was highly amusing, out of the night sky appeared "Bed Check Charlie," known to the soldiers by that name because almost every night at about this time a lone German pilot would traverse this area to see what was going on with the American troops. We were too far back to draw artillery fire but there was always the possibility that he could drop a few bombs, but none of the battle hardened GIs got very excited about his presence. Everyone just sat there and smoked, laughed, and watched the show, until the rear echelon officers in charge of the show got jittery and decided to cancel the rest of the show, including the movie. The men on the hills roared their disapproval but to no effect. Not one combat GI got up and left the area but watched in disbelief as the officers and enlisted men of special service hurriedly took down the stage, dismantled their spotlight, loaded their trucks with all the stage paraphernalia, and grabbed Mr. Bogart and his wife, putting them into a jeep and hurriedly driving away amid a tremendous outpouring of boos emanating from the GIs. Even the German pilot must have been surprised; he probably wanted to get a glimpse of the show. But most rear echeloners are psycho cases when they get too close to the front; this was another case of how they had made fools not only of themselves, but of poor Humphrey Bogart.

The fellows who had come to the show at my urging now were telling me it was the last time anyone was going to listen to my opinions concerning U.S.O. shows put out by the rear echelon special services, and it was the last time the outfit was entertained by the U.S.O., though we had another twenty months of overseas duty. The respect that was evidenced at the beginning of the performance for him seemed to dissolve into the darkness of the night as his jeep sped down the darkened road carrying the print of his latest movie further and further away from the hungry eyes of the GIs left behind on the rolling Italian hill.

Trying to remember Humphrey Bogart in his role in *Casablanca* was a consoling thought at that time but it brought out one point that movie heroes are like yesterday's newspapers, of no consequence.

The division had been in the rest area for a little over two weeks when a notice was put on the bulletin board that the division had been alerted and was to get ready to move out for further adventure. It was placed next to the letter to the division signed by General Clark when the division first arrived at the rest area stating that the division was in for a long and well-deserved rest. Laughing, the men denounced General Clark while reading the latest notice, with some remarking that generals couldn't be trusted anymore than the Germans.

Loaded onto trucks and whisked away, not back to the mountains, but south toward Naples; however, not to Naples as everyone had hoped. The trucks drove into an area near what was called the racetrack—down and down into an area that seemed to have been a dead volcano. Another rumor spread that this place had once been the hunting grounds of the king of Naples, so what the hell were we doing here?

On the ride from Venafro to our new bivouac area, my mind was filled with incidents that had happened before the regiment had been relieved. I thought, how foolish Sergeant Rerter had been when he thought a battlefield commission would be given to him. All those chances he took, for one whose fear of enemy fire was very discernible. He sure wanted that commission real bad. Yet a lieutenant had been sent to take over the platoon; he took the place of Lieutenant Rant, who was no great loss. Unlike Lieutenant Rant, who came from the South, the new Lieutenant was from New York. He had been a policeman there. The day he came up to our company, another lieutenant had come along with him named Lieutenant Nolso, who hailed from the Midwest. Both of these lieutenants spent a few days in Sergeant Rerter's company and his psycho condition seemed to be catching. Lieutenant Nolso was sent to I Company, but he didn't stay there long; he was back with Lieutenant Lorid and Sergeant Rerter. Poor guy, he was no more than twenty or so. Back in the States a commission was a big thing even if it was in the infantry. On the line an officer's rank was more or less a detriment as leadership had to be shown or one's rank was as important as the mud encountered in a foxhole. Lieutenant Nolso left his position and refused to go back up; he had been on the line for less than a week. He was sent back to the rear with the baggage, and just before we boarded the trucks, someone told us that he had shot himself and committed suicide. It was hard to believe; that was the last that was heard of him, but it was a lesson that new men should never be put in the company of those soldiers in combat who were a little battle weary and had time to strike fear in one's mind before that person had even a chance to engage in combat.

Down into this volcano-like forest the trucks descended. Coming to a halt everyone got out. Looking around, we couldn't see very far as there was a heavy layer of fog blanketing the whole area. Walking carefully as we were directed to our area, swamplike ground gave way under our feet. Finally as our platoon came to a halt we were told to set up tents in the area. This was accomplished without much trouble; no one bitched at this outrageous place. The main reason was that there was no enemy shooting at us; every soldier knew that as long as we stayed in this miserable place we would be safe for a little while longer. So as the days passed into a week everyone just laid around and bullshitted as the troops were completely cut off from the outside world, except for the radios that the communication section were outfitted with.

One day one soldier who I had been fairly friendly with came over and told me two other friends of his wanted to talk to me. Going over to them, I kept wondering what they wanted to know and what the hell could I tell them—after all, there wasn't any information coming into the area as to where the division was headed next. Though these men weren't close friends they had a certain respect for my integrity and intelligence. Sitting down on what dry ground could be found in this swampy area, I asked what was so important that they wanted to discuss in this miserable place.

"We're going to shoot ourselves," two of them uttered in unison.

"What the hell do you want to do that for?" I asked, startled.

The three of them told me that they had heard that the division was headed for another amphibious invasion and that they couldn't take it anymore.

"What the hell do you want me for?" I asked. "Besides, you can't do that. Take your chances with the rest of us. Don't be fools. You've come this far; you're kidding anyway. Why are you telling me this?"

"We respect you and besides we thought that you might like to join us."

"I haven't got the guts to shoot myself and besides I'll take my chances with the enemy." I tried to talk reason into them and I thought I was successful as they seemed to be changing their minds. With another warning not to be foolish, I walked away feeling that my conversation had deterred their plan.

CHAPTER ELEVEN

Anzio

The next morning I was awakened by Hook shaking my shoulder, "I just heard where we're going next," he yelled excitedly.

"Where?" I asked.

"Anzio," he replied. "I was listening to the news on the radio and there was an announcement that Allied troops had just landed about 30 miles south of Rome." So it was another amphibious assault that we were going to be part of, but the initial assault had already taken place. At least our division wasn't going to be the first on the beach this time.

The mess sergeant had started serving breakfast. Hot coffee felt good, but no one lingered around the mess tent. Off to the area where the communication platoon was located was where most of us headed to eat our breakfast while we listened to the latest news on the radio. It was the morning of January 22 and as everyone crowded around the radio on the back of the jeep, someone said quietly, "Here we go again." Listening to the details of the invasion as given out by the BBC, we heard "Allied troops have landed on Anzio 30 miles south of Rome with very little opposition." When the men heard that, a cheer emanated from the crowd, for that meant the invasion forces would be far inland by time our regiment landed. As we listened, BBC news started giving out the different units that had landed at Anzio: Ranger battalions, 3rd Division, 1st British Division—all units that we had become familiar with. They were good combat units. They might be in Rome before we landed there. At least everyone hoped so. Thus through the radio was our next destination given to us; it had to be Anzio—not Casino. The generals wouldn't have brought us all the way back to the Naples area and then sent us back the same way the division had come. Was it really Anzio?

Two days later I found myself on a LST (landing ship tank) heading north. The company had been thrown together with different units; there were trucks from the service company, parts or an artillery battery, and even a rifle company. The generals had decided to get as many men to this new combat area as soon as possible so the ship traveled through the Mediterranean Sea. I got myself into the back of one of the trucks and went to sleep as darkness came, not to be awakened until almost dawn by the ringing out of a rifle shot that seemed to come from the hold of the ship. The first sound of a rifle shot was followed by a second and then a third. For a minute it seemed that the ship was under small arms fire. Then I remembered those three men out of my company who had invited me to shoot myself when they did. Could they have actually done it? It couldn't be; someone must have accidentally fired his rifle.

The ship was still moving and it wasn't quite light. I went back to sleep, but was awakened a second time by voices that kept yelling, "Medics, someone's shot." Those fools—did they really shoot themselves? Those men really had an abnormal fear of what German firepower could do to them. Could they have been prophetic about the future—settling for a wound that would take them out or action rather than waiting to be blown to bits or going completely psycho? How could they know about what would happen on Anzio? Churchill later was quoted as saying, "If there's a hell on earth it has to be Anzio!"

This time I got out of the back of the truck and started to move around when a voice came over the ship's loudspeaker announcing that the ship was about to hit the beach and everyone should prepare to get off with his unit.

This was my third invasion and the fourth ship that I had been on since leaving the States, but the first time that a hot cup of coffee hadn't been served to the men before leaving for the beach. Even condemned criminals are given a last meal, but not infantry men. It seems that those in command always treat their most valuable possession with the least care.

Sergeant Rerter came by and told the men to get into any of the trucks as they were all going in one direction and when they stopped, the men could wait by the trucks and the company would be assembled. I wasn't about to get into a truck before it got down the ramp of the LST. Artillery shells could be coming onto the beach; there was always the chance of an air raid. So a few of us decided to walk off the LST, following the truck that was supposed to carry us to our destination. Slowly the line moved off the ramp onto the beach and up the road leading away from it. Everything moved quietly but slowly so there was no problem walking along with the line of trucks. A few incoming shells could be seen breaking a few hundred yards up the road. For an invasion, it was rather quiet even though this was the third day that the beachhead had been established.

As we walked along, my mind went back to the shots that had been fired on the ship. Had those three men that had taken me into their confidence really shot themselves? If so, hadn't they been foolish? This was an easy invasion—hardly any enemy opposition as we walked alongside the trucks.There was only a misty dreary morning, the kind of morning that one would like to get in out of the rain into a nice dry house. In place of the house, the undercarriage of the truck body was used as protection from the elements. While waiting for Sergeant Rerter to come by to assemble our platoon, I didn't dare get up into the back of the truck as it was too vulnerable for any shrapnel that might be flying about even though there were only a few shells being directed at us by the enemy.

Once assembled, the few of us that belonged to the same platoon got into the jeep that Sergeant Rerter had come for us in and drove away in a northwestern direction for about five miles to where the rest of the company was bivouacked. Waiting for the battalion to get in place, a few shells were falling in the immediate vicinity; it was nothing for anyone to get excited about so there weren't any foxholes dug. Everyone just lay around enjoying the mild late January weather.

For a full week, the regiment stayed in its original position with the troops just lolling around and being entertained every day at sunset by German bombers that tried to drop their bombs back at the harbors of Nettuno and Anzio. Every gun on the beachhead opened up on the enemy planes from the regular antiaircraft guns onshore and the ships offshore to the machine guns mounted on the tanks, jeeps, trucks, and even the machine guns of the heavy weapons companies as the German bombers came into sight. Rifles were even fired at the targets, or sitting ducks, as these planes seemed to move with a slowness of a World War I tank. One by one, the bombers were shot out of the sky, falling like lighted torches, to be swallowed up by the sea. This continued for a full week and was the highlight of the day as thousands of bullets and shells filled the sky as darkness was about to fall. It made the area seem like the Fourth of July was being celebrated every night for a week. The bombers traveled in single file as they came in on their bombing run and their silver bodies shone brightly as the late afternoon sun reflected off these slowly moving planes that only a few years earlier had been the scourge of most of the countries of Europe. As they were shot down one at a time from the outpouring of firepower from the beachhead, I wondered how they could have scared so many millions of people into surrender? Watching this entertainment in the late afternoon made me think that it was no different from watching a ball game at Yankee Stadium, only instead of yelling "Kill the Umpire," we yelled, "Kill the Nazi bastards."

The fighter planes of the German Air Force; for example, such as the Messerschmidts were a different story, for they came right out of the sun for their strafing and bombing runs and were a little harder to knock out of the sky than the antiquated German bombers. There was a squadron of American fighter planes operating out of Naples that gave the beachhead protection against the German fighter planes; they were P-47's (Thunderbolts) manned by an all-Black crew and were a top-notch fighter outfit. Even though there were many bigoted men in the division, the cheers emanating from their throats every time a German plane was shot down by the Black pilots was unequaled by any cheering that I had ever heard. And shoot down the Nazi bastards they did! One of the Black pilots was a lieutenant by the name of Davis. Later he was to go on to become a general in the Air Corps. A few times the Nazis bombed the hospital and some nurses were killed and wounded. The word would spread to the front whenever the hospital was bombed. The grumbling would get louder and louder from the men so when an enemy plane was shot down and the pilot parachuted out, he would usually land among the troops on the beach. Whenever this happened, MPs would be seen riding in their jeeps to the position where the enemy pilot had come down, not to pick him up, but to get to the front lines before the troops on the line could get to the German pilot and kill him as the American troops' wrath was unbounded at the criminal action of the German pilots' bombing of the hospital. So it was a race between the front line troops and the MPs for the Nazi pilots.

The only reason the MPs (military Police) were still able to come up to the front with abandon was that the enemy firepower hadn't been brought into full intensity and the few enemy shells that fell were just enough to let everyone know that the Nazis had a few tanks out on the hills above us.

The MPs were booed roundly as they put the German pilots in their jeep and rode the long gauntlet through the front line troops to the rear; no one attempted to relieve them of their captured enemy as they drove the hated pilots along a circuitous road back to the rear. The booing could be heard all over the beachhead as the troops derided them for protecting these hated Nazi sons of bitches.

The first week went by with everyone just hanging around. The

Alban hills to the East looked so clean and it made everyone wonder why no attempt had been made to advance to these hills as there was practically no enemy activity in the vicinity. In the past when the enemy had all kinds of firepower to throw down on the troops, the word to advance was handed down. Here at Anzio, with very little opposition the troops were held on a leash. The first axiom learned at any military school is to take the high ground; one wondered what military school our generals had gone to. Later we found out it was West Point. Where else?

During that first week of hanging around, not even digging in, with the main entertainment the bombing raids, I was inclined to walk over to the communication platoon to listen to their radio and hear the news emanating from BBC.

Listening to the radio, which was situated on the back of the communication section's jeep, had become an early-evening ritual, and the news was listened to most intently. First, there would be the number of air raids that the RAF (Royal Air Force) had performed and the damage they had done; then the sorties flown by the American Air Force and the damage done.Next we listened to the doings of the Russian army and how far they had advanced. The Russians were on the move and here we Allied troops were at a standstill. So when I made a few disparaging remarks about our generals, Sergeant Hightower, the communication platoon sergeant took me up on my argument and told me that the Russians weren't the only ones fighting the war, as my remarks had seemed to imply, and that the Americans were right in the middle of it doing their part even if it didn't seem that we weren't doing much at the time. He was right, but I didn't let him know it. I never could get it through my mind that we surely were in the forefront of the action; I was like someone watching a war movie and thinking the other guys were the soldiers and I was just a spectator. I never did get a chance to apologize to Sergeant Hightower for my words at that time, for it wasn't too long after that he was killed in action.

When the newscaster mentioned the Allied troops on Anzio, he said they were securing the beachhead. If he had been told the truth about us just sitting around when Rome could have been taken during the first two days, Generals Clark and Alexander would have been relieved of their command.

About the ninth day, the all-Black P-47s squadron seemed to be overhead constantly. Didn't they have to go back to Naples to refuel? I wondered. Someone told me a small airfield had been built on Anzio where the pilots were able to land and refuel, thus giving the beachhead excellent protection against enemy planes. One didn't hear any derogatory remarks about Blacks on that beachhead.

The next morning, I was awakened by the whistle of enemy artillery shells going overhead toward the beach. What's going on? The Germans have finally got an army down here to throw us off the beach. Were our generals working for the Germans? It sure seemed like it.

The battalion was moved over to an area closer to the water and more to the south; no one was told why. There we bivouacked for about two days where we could watch the German planes come in at night to drop bombs on the ships in the harbor and, of course, as the Nazis were known as gentlemen, they had to bomb a hospital ship, setting it on fire even though this ship of mercy had all its lights on as the international conventions of war demanded. Watching this ship burn through the night from a few miles inland gave us a sinking sensation. Certainly it proved that even the German Air Corps officers, who considered themselves above the ordinary Nazi dogs, were just as depraved.

Watching an air attack the following night, one of the German fighter bomber planes was hit by antiaircraft fire and set ablaze in the darkened sky. Then the pilot swung the plane around and turned the nose of the plane downward, heading for the ships in the harbor and looking like a fiery comet. This Nazi bastard was committing suicide, but he was going to take a ship with him and as many of the Allied personnel as he could. This was the first time I had seen such a suicidal run; later, when hearing of the Japanese Kamikaze pilots,

I realized the Germans were just as dedicated to their idiot leader as the Japanese were. Only the Nazi bastards did it first. The Nazi plane headed for one ship, hitting it and setting the ship on fire with a loud explosion, lighting up the entire harbor, exposing the unloading of the tons of supplies for the beachhead, and making this area a good target for the enemy planes bombing that night. It was one of the few times that I was glad that I wasn't in theNavy or part of the rear echelon that was in supply.

Our platoon set up around a stone house in the area where a few civilians were still in evidence. The lieutenant had bartered a few bottles of wine which he dispersed among us; it was the last alcoholic drink that I was to have until Rome was captured. The wine was more vinegar than wine, but who cared? As we drank out in the open, night had started to fall and as I looked out over the landscape there was a patrol in single file going by not 25 yards away. Could it be the enemy? Who else? No one bothered to challenge the patrol, including the lieutenant. Why should I? Everyone continued to drink even though my finger pointed in the general direction of the patrol.

The next day the company was alerted before dawn, and marched to an area where there was a deep ditch called the Mussolini Canal. Why it was called a canal was beyond me as it was devoid of any water. The battalion was told to take up a defensive position so everyone dug in; it was the first time that I had dug a foxhole since arriving at Anzio. Things were quiet, but the lieutenant took a few of us on a patrol across the canal to reconnoiter the area. This was the same lieutenant who had arrived in our unit after Venafro and was a little psycho back there. Most of it was brought on by Sergeant Rerter's nervous condition at the time. So it seemed that he had recovered from his nervousness. If he had only known that the regiment had been ordered to cover this area because three ranger battalions had been almost wiped out in a belated attack at the German lines only a day earlier.

The battalion remained at this position for a few days; thus, giving me a little time to dream in my foxhole about the past seven months since the division had left the States. I was laughing to myself as I remembered seeing Mussolini's famous tanks in Sicily for the first time. Everyone had been led to believe that Mussolini's armor was formidable, but when I saw that a rifle bullet could go right through the steel that was supposed to have protected his tanks, I realized what a wonderful job his Fascist publicity agents had done to make the world believe he had superior fighting forces, when his armies surrendered to whomever they could find and his tanks could be knocked out with a rifle.

As I reminisced, these two tough line company captains came to my mind—Captain Beggs and Captain Conrady, whose companies (K and I) I had been assigned to in Sicily. Both were killed at Salerno. What a shame! They were two top-fighting Americans. Lieutenant Russo who had been killed at Salerno was one of the few officers that I had really liked and respected. Sergeant Harris who had been killed at Filignano, was a nice guy, but what good had all that sleight-of-hand business at cards done him? It made me think; maybe principles should make up one's character and there should be no deterring from them. But Lieutenant Russo, whose principles had gotten him railroaded out of our company by the Okies, was dead, killed in action because of those principles. So which way does one go? As I looked out at the landscape around me, I saw scallions coming out of the ground in early February. That was something that the winters in Connecticut didn't produce. Winters were mild at Anzio south of Rome.

Principles could get one in trouble. Felix Subverri had gotten into an argument with the company commander and his executive officer on a matter of principle while we had been hanging around the beachhead after the first week. He had been transferred to a line company. Those two officers should have been transferred, not Subvervi, but then there's so much one can take. The argument was around some cattle that had been immobilized by the company and then butchered right in the company's front yard, but the division of the meat was in question. Subvervi, thinking the men should get a greater share of the meat than was being allotted by the officers, got into a position where he could only lose. After being transferred to I Company, Subvervi was captured by the Germans a few weeks later during their offensive to drive the American troops off the beachhead. These same two officers also made what Okies were left in the company mad at them. Captain Nan and Lieutenant Hun had picked a newcomer to the company to go home on the first rotation plan allotted to the division overseas. Their claim was that this soldier was overseas longer than anyone else in the company and that he had been in North Africa six months before the division had arrived in Africa. The fact that he had been in a noncombatant outfit and had never seen any action didn't faze these two officers, but they were brazen enough to pull this caper off; it was hard to understand. I wouldn't have even been considered to go, so why should I get involved? Let the Okies take it out on these two. Ugly rumors had gone around that he had given the captain $1,000 that he had won in a card game or that he had been involved in the black market in Africa; thus, he was shipped to an infantry outfit as punishment. The only one who really got hurt by all of this was Felix Subvervi; poor Felix also became an ex-corporal like me.

After a few days by the Mussolini Canal, the company was alerted and again the regiment moved over to an area known as the factory. Our company was located in what seemed to be a farm development. There were barns for cattle and the opening was bounded by two towers of solid stonework; it seemed like it was an entrance to an old castle. Inside one of the towers, a British detachment occupied the ground area; they were the troops we were supposed to relieve. The story was going around that the British First Division had gotten to Campoleone 16 miles from Rome and some of its forward elements had gotten as far as the outskirts of the Holy City, but had taken a bad mauling from the Germans. Our division had been alerted to take over the sector they had occupied while the British division had a chance to regroup. The regiment had no sooner gotten to this new area than the German artillery started to flow in at an accelerated rate that made it most uncomfortable to stay above ground.

The company adjusted itself to this new environment—cattle smells all over the place, and civilian refugees occupying the barns until they could be transported back to the rear. Walking into one of the barns where I was going to sleep, Italian civilians occupied most of the straw that was laid out on the floor. Almost falling down on the straw out of sheer exhaustion, I was kept awake most of the night by the moans and groans of the civilians, whom I first thought were making these strange utterances because of their fear, but found out to my amusement that sex was the reason for those horrible sounds. Those Italians—even if the world was being destroyed; they would be promiscuous.

Falling asleep was an easy matter even though the thunder and lightning around the barnyard was man-made and not God made.

The next day, the civilians were evacuated from our area. Later I learned that all civilians had been evacuated from the beachhead. How I envied them; but there was good reason for their evacuation. The army would have had to feed them, and the civilians would have gotten in the way. Many would have been killed and wounded. Extra medical care would have been directed to their needs, probably leaving a shortage of medical care for the men already there.

The next night Rerter woke me up. He told me I would have to accompany a service company truck driver named Lyons back to the rear to pick up a load of ammunition for the battalion. Not taking that order lying down, I railed at Rerter to pick someone else as I had been on guard duty most of the night. Of course, my protest was in vain and I found myself riding shotgun on a two-and-a-half-ton truck down the road toward the beachhead where the ammunition dump was located. The ride back to the port was uneventful or so it seemed as I was still drowsy from having been awakened after dropping off to sleep, so I didn't pay much attention to the flashes in the sky or along the roadside. If my senses had been completely with me, experience would have warned me that artillery was dropping alongside the narrow road. Of course unknown to me, the Germans had broken through our lines and many of our units were under severe enemy fire from front and rear.

Lyons was a good truck driver; he kept going, and soon our destination was reached. The ammunition dump was easy to locate as it was lit up as brightly as Times Square, and the only difference was the lack of electric signs.

German artillery had set parts of the ammunition dump on fire; other parts of the ammunition dump had been set on fire by incendiary bombs from the night bombing of the German air force. In fact, they were still overhead when we arrived. Jumping from the truck, Lyons and I quickly looked around for some underground shelter or someone to direct us to some dugout. Just ahead was a tent. Running to the tent in desperation, we hoped to find someone there, but it was empty as a politician's promises. My combat experience hadn't been in vain; my nose could smell out a cellar, dugout, foxhole, or any kind of shelter that was below artillery level. Not more than 15 yards from the tent, a conelike dugout loomed up out of the brightness of the surrounding fires and exploding shells which made it seem like a Fourth of July celebration back home. The German artillery and Air Force were certainly having a field day. They seemed to have a competition going between them to see which arm of the Nazi military could set off the most fires in an American ammunition dump.

There was a sergeant in the dugout who was in charge of about a dozen men with him. The flicker of a few candles was the only light in the dugout. Their faces seemed to have been painted with the whitest of white paint; not one word came out of these men. Who could blame them? It was bad enough being under an artillery and bombing attack at the same time, but to have your own artillery shells exploding all over the place was a little too much. Knowing how tense these men were, I spoke softly to the sergeant telling him that our battalion was almost out of ammunition and that the battalion needed a load of small-arms ammunition and mortar shells.

The sergeant didn't move and as I wasn't in any hurry to get outside with the fireworks, it seemed like a good time to sit down and have a smoke. Slowly the men started talking, asking what the situation was up on the line, and that was not much better than back here. I thought to myself: here were a bunch of guys who thought they had a pretty safe job in the army. Way back in the rear, all they had to do was load ammunition on the trucks that came into their supply dump and cart the ammunition anywhere from 20 to 25 miles to a position near the front lines where it was distributed to regimental supply dumps. Here at Anzio the front lines had been compressed so that the rear was only six miles from the front. It was doubtful that these men had been under enemy fire before even though as I found out, most had been overseas for more than six months.

It was almost midnight and an hour had gone by since our arrival; the bombing had stopped and thinking it was time to load up the truck before it was blown to bits by enemy shells or our own that were exploding all over the place, it seemed a good time to make a move.

Telling the sergeant it was time to move and load up, I crawled up out of the dugout followed by Lyons, the sergeant, and about half of his men. Once outside the sergeant seemed to have regained his courage and told us to follow him with the truck, he led us over to an area where the small arms ammunition was stored.

The sky was still lit up with the fires from the ammo dump, but the bombing had stopped. The men started to load the truck at a fierce pace, for which they couldn't be blamed. It was worse than playing Russian roulette as exploding shells from the dump would set fire to different piles for ammunition and shrapnel continued to fly in all directions. How we ever got out of there alive still remains a mystery. The truck was half loaded when the drone of aircraft rose above the noise of the exploding shells; the German bastards were back. The sons of bitches dropped flares to light up the area; it was like lighting up a flashlight in Yankee Stadium during a night game. The fires were bright enough to see the target, so the flares were psychological, more to scare the hell out of the men on the ground. The flares did the job. They scared the hell out of the men loading the truck and off they ran to their hole in the ground, leaving Dave Lyons and me to finish loading the truck. The bombs started to come down and the whistles from the bombs descending were enough to turn one's blood to water and then to shit, which one usually did when night bombing took place right over one's head or so it seemed.

With the most alacrity on our part the loading of the truck was finished, and then through the exploding shells in the ammunition dump our truck weaved its way. Why shrapnel didn't tear the truck apart was beyond me. But my thoughts weren't of the shrapnel, but just to get out of this area. We started on the road back to our battalion's position, which was covered with exploding shells thrown in by the miserable Nazi bastards. We got out of the truck when we were waved down by soldiers standing in the road. They wanted to know where we were going. They were British troops who had been pushed back from their positions and had set up a defensive line on the south side of the road, telling us this was the front and the road was in no-mans land.

The truck literally slowed down to a crawl as I walked in front of the truck slowly feeling our way over the shell holes strewn around in front or the blacked out lights of the truck. Tracer bullets from machine guns were now traversing the road adding to the fiery display of exploding shells; it would have been a wonderful sight to have watched from five miles away, but one lucky shot on the truck and that ammunition would go up into a fiery display that would not have been equaled by anything that had occurred in my experience thus far.

Lighting up a cigarette and using it as a torch so Lyons could follow me as he drove the truck, we went yard by yard until the enemy started to light up the road with flares. It was becoming too dangerous to go along at this slow pace. Jumping back into the truck, I told Lyons to pick up the speed a bit and pick his way as best he could. With the light from the flares it became easier to see the holes and bumps in the road and also for the enemy to see the truck.

Finally, the towers of the castle could be made out as enemy shells exploding off the stone turrets lit up the immediate vicinity for a few seconds and then darkness prevailed for another second or two before the area was alight again. It seemed as if someone was playing with an electric light switch. Accelerating the truck to a speed of around twenty miles an hour from the ten miles or so that the truck had been traveling, Lyons brought the truck into the courtyard and between the towers safely. Jumping out of the truck and running into company headquarters, I informed the company commander and then Sergeant Rerter that the ammunition had arrived; whereupon, Rerter told both of us to go to bed and he would have the platoon unload the truck.

Going into the barn to lie down, I found it to be full of civilians, who hadn't gotten a chance to get back to the rear and were caught in the German offensive. Exhausted, I lay down in the dark almost tripping over some civilians who were in a passionate embrace. How the hell could anyone think of sex at a time like this? All hell had broken loose, bombs were whistling down from the darkened sky, shells were bursting off the walls of the castle, even the tracer bullets from the enemy machine guns sped silently through the night around this complex and here were these Italian civilians on a romantic foray.

Tired to a point of exhaustion, sleep came easily with fear of the enemy firepower receding as quickly as it took my eyes to close. I was awakened in a few minutes by someone yelling out my name. It was a new man in the platoon, a replacement who had come in just before Anzio. He was demanding to know why Rerter hadn't awakened me to help unload the truck. A miserable private who hadn't seen a week of action was demanding to know why I wasn't awakened to help with this chore. Before I could arise, Rerter laced into him telling him that I had brought the truck in after having been gone five hours looking for the ammunition dump. Not only did I deserve the rest, but the next time this private opened his mouth he would find himself in a rifle company.

The next morning all the ammunition was distributed to all the companies in the battalion who were getting ready for a counterattack for the following morning. There was no treat for me as I was put on guard duty behind the castle with two other men from the platoon. The next night, around five in the morning, all hell broke loose. If the previous night had been a nightmare, there wasn't any description to be given to this enemy offensive. It seemed as if all the German firepower had been put in a giant cement mixer, rolled around a few times, and then opened up, spewing forth a mixture of bombs, shells, and bullets of all kinds that shook the earth with as much power as two earthquakes joining forces with a couple of volcanoes and going off at the same time.

Excited voices could be heard in the courtyard from our position in the rear of the complex yelling out orders to get all the men to defensive positions around the castle. Luckily, the civilians had been moved out the previous day. Running to the front of the castle where a defensive line had been set up with a couple of machine guns already in position to cover the enemy's flank, everyone lay down in the ditch that ran parallel to the road and waited for the enemy. There was no enemy but the remnants of one of the line companies came out of the early morning mist. Then some more men from another company came straggling through our position and continued to a destination in the rear. Not long after, an order was given to our company to retreat down the road over which I had come with the load of ammunition the previous night.

Strung out over the road, what was left of the battalion retreated slowly as tracer bullets from enemy machine guns competed for space on the same road with the retreating soldiers. Two nights before, the British troops had been pushed back to this same road a few miles to the west of our position. Now it seemed that our next defensive position would be on the south side of this same road. There remained a question in my mind; how far would we retreat? After all, it was only five miles to the water. Still the retreat was orderly, not as if the troops were running from the enemy, but knowing we had to reorganize, slowly moved backward, daring the enemy to come at us if they dared. Finally, about a half mile south of the road that had been the lifeline to our position, the troops came to a halt and were told to dig in on a knoll overlooking the road that we had just come from. Really it was more like a country road, just wide enough to handle one-way traffic. How tanks, trucks, and troops were able to make such use of this parcel of road without tearing it to pieces was a tribute to the Italians who had built this road. This was something they were masters of, and anywhere one traveled throughout Italy one could perceive that their road-building was an art.

Relaxing for a moment or two in the cold February weather while lying in a quickly dug foxhole, my rest was interrupted by the company commander, who was standing nearby, calling Sergeant Rerter over and telling him to send some men down to the road to direct any stragglers from the battalion who were able to escape to the position on top of the knoll where the battalion was now encamped.

Why did he call Rerter? This was a job for the intelligence section, not the A&P platoon. Rerter wasted no time in getting a volunteer to take up this detail, for the first name that came to his mind was mine. All the other sergeants, assistant squad leaders, and other ass wipers seemed to always get eliminated when a dangerous job came up. Not one other man did he order to go along with me. Why he always took pleasure in ordering me to a dangerous job was easily comprehensible. My mind always went back to the Venafro area when he asked me to go back to the rear command post and I refused preferring to stay with the forward CP. Ever since, he had been on my back. Maybe it was because I didn't show the fear that he had shown.

I walked down to the road listening for any unusual sounds that might be in the air. Then over my head came a welcome sound, the whirr of our artillery that seemed to be on an invisible road overhead, sounding like heavy trucks speeding by. Then as the artillery barrage got heavier it sounded like locomotives racing each other on railroad tracks that ran parallel to each other in the clouds overhead that seemed to stand motionless in the sky.

Getting closer to the road, the artillery shells going overhead toward the enemy seemed to be coming back down. One could almost follow their direction by the whoosh emanating from each artillery shell as they sped by. A few tracer bullets were still coming across the road from the machine guns of the Nazi bastards. The road looked deserted as I approached my destinations. What the hell was I doing here alone? What if a wave of Germans came over that hill? Do I fight back or surrender? I would possibly be killed once they saw the "H" on my dog tags. Surrender was definitely out of the question. While thinking, my mind must have blanked out because almost in front of me appeared another American soldier. He looked just as glad to see me as I was to see him. We smiled at each other, realizing that neither of us would be alone if the enemy came charging over that hill.

There was a contrast in our ranks. I had just been made a PFC by an act of Congress, and he was a Major. After we greeted each other, he told me he was looking for stragglers from his battalion which was the second battalion from my regiment. (My battalion was the third.)

After telling him I was looking for stragglers from my battalion, I offered him a cigarette and we both lit up, all the time looking up and over the road. We were facing the enemy positions. We were both holding our carbines at the ready with one hand as we looked for stragglers from our battalions, but we looked even harder for any enemy soldiers that might suddenly appear. As the minutes went by, the tension eased and we started talking as long-lost friends do after being separated for a long time. He told me he had taken command of the battalion when the battalion commander had been incapacitated and what was left of his battalion had retreated and was trying to reform in a small hollow that lay a few hundred yards behind us. What was mystifying to me was why the battalion commander was out trying to find stragglers when he could have delegated this task to anyone in his battalion. Here was I a lowly PFC sent out alone on a miserable job like this. Instead of sending an officer, the bastards had sent me! I was expendable to those yellow bastards in command of my company. Why didn't the major think the same way? What a difference in men! He was looking out for his men personally, and if anyone was going to got killed on this mission, it was going to be him.

I could see he wanted to get back to his battalion after being in this position for about an hour, but he was too honorable to make the first move. I made the first move by asking him if he didn't have to get back to his battalion since he was the commander. I also mentioned that it didn't look like any stragglers were coming back this way. Our position was strengthened by the artillery barrage that was being laid down by all the artillery our side could muster, from the destroyers and cruisers of the American and British Navy offshore with their 4-, 6-, and 8-inch naval guns to the 155-, 105-millimeter artillery pieces or the Army, and the 90-millimeter pieces on the tanks that laid down a steady stream of steel that burst upon the enemy with devastating results. One would have to say this rain of steel was one of the main reasons the Germans' attack was slowed down.

After lighting up another cigarette, the major reluctantly told me he had to get back to his battalion. Of course, I understood. He should never have been out here with me. He shook hands with me as he left. Watching him move across the fields and down into the hollow, I suddenly realized that there wasn't anyone in this immediate area but me. Half the firepower that had been in this section had disappeared when the Major left. What was I still doing here? All the fireworks were going over my head in both directions, so at the moment it didn't seem to be the worst place in the world to be, unless some German troops suddenly appeared on the road. However, it seemed time to leave and head back to what was left of the third battalion, report that no stragglers had come across the road—and if they didn't believe me, they could go look themselves. Making my way back across the open fields, I heard a roar; it wasn't exploding shells, but human voices that thundered up from the hollow where the major from the second battalion had gone.

Looking down into the hollow, an unusual sight came into view. Soldiers running at a fast pace toward the road with bayonets fixed, yelling at the tops of their lungs, and in the forefront was the Major. It was an awesome sight, something one would expect to see in the movies where men always seemed to be willing to die for their country, but here was the real thing. About four hundred men charging into the mouth of oblivion, almost like the Charge of the Light Brigade, only these men weren't riding horses. One might see opposing football teams come roaring into a field in this manner just before a game started, but not into the deadly fire of the enemy. Though I stood stunned while watching this, a surge of pride came over me. Here were American soldiers acting heroically in an almost hopeless situation, and I was part of this army; that was a moment when I was proud to be an American.

I never did learn the Major's name, or whether he was killed, wounded, or came out alive. There were people whose names were known to me and their name and their person has been forgotten, but never shall I forget the Major leading those men in that charge at Anzio.

Once the charging soldiers were out of sight, I continued back to my battalion where everything was still in disorder with some of the officers trying to set up a defensive line on the high ground overlooking the battlefield with the three hundred or so men left in the battalion from the nine hundred men that had been part of the battalion the night before.

Walking back to join my platoon, sitting on a slight ridge just beyond two machine guns was Dave Cavanaugh from New London. He was a machine gun sergeant, so it wasn't unusual for him to be with a machine gun section, but I had heard that he had been wounded and was back in the hospital down by the beach. This was a surprise! What was he doing here when he could be enjoying the white sheets, hot food, and safety of the hospital? He had to be a damn fool to come back up to the line, especially at this time. His forehead had a bandage and his lip had some sort of bandage, a sure reason to be kept out of action. He told me that it was safer at the front than it was in the hospital. Artillery shells were exploding all over the area where the hospital was located, and what planes the Germans still had were dropping bombs all over the beach and that was where the hospital was located, and one couldn't dig in a hospital bed like one could dig a hole at the front. Besides, he told me, orders had been given that every hospitalized soldier who could move be sent back up to the lines.

He asked me how it looked from where I had come. I told him it was all confusion, but our men were still holding out and that I had just talked to a soldier in the communication section that an order had come down from division headquarters that there was to be no retreat from the position that we now held. Where the hell could one go, unless one went swimming into the Tyrrhenian Sea?

The next day a few of us from our platoon were called up to move down the road where I had been the day before to dig in to the side of the embankment in order to set up a communication center for a forward CP. At first, I thought it was going to be for the battalion colonel, but to my surprise up walked the regimental colonel with the division general. They were going to watch the battle from this vantage point, or so they thought. Alongside the road there were about six tanks with their 90-millimeter guns hanging over the side of the embankment and firing away at will. Then Colonel Kammerer and General Eagles pulled out their field glasses and watched the battle with the rest of us. In between, we dug out an enlarged foxhole, watching the Germans advancing and ducking the incoming artillery. It seemed like another day at Anzio, except that the regimental colonel and division general were in the audience alongside us.

Incoming shells were almost as frequent as those that were fired by our artillery and as they passed overhead, a couple of the fellows got nervous and hit the ground. One of them was named Sertal; he hit the ground even when it was our shells going overhead. The general and colonel noticed his actions and tried to calm him down. Here were two officers of the division showing concern for one of the ordinary soldiers while they were trying to direct a battle. I tried to get Sertal to get into our makeshift command post, so he wouldn't make us all nervous.

The enemy shelling was getting heavier and as I looked over the embankment I could see the German troops starting to overrun our line company's positions. The men in the tanks also saw this and, to my surprise, out of their tanks they came, beating a hasty retreat to the rear. The Germans weren't upon us yet; Colonel Kammerer and General Eagles watched the tank men run away and seemed as stunned as I. Then the colonel and general took off in a jeep that had been waiting for them down the road.

There was no order to retreat but men were moving back in all directions. There wasn't even a noncom in our group to give an order to evacuate, but the CP we had dug out looked pretty good to stay in for a while, which we did until a lieutenant from another company came by and told us we better get out of that position and get back to the rear where the battalion was located.

Back at the battalion CP, it was almost as if what was left of the battalion was encamped in one area—probably no more than two hundred men. Everyone seemed listless and a defensive line had been set up for what would probably be a last stand. After digging in as best we could in an exhausted condition, everyone relaxed and waited.

The next day there was an unusual amount of activity about 30 yards beyond our position. Soldiers walked back to where there was a low position and disappeared down a knoll. Wondering what was going on, I got out of my hole and followed a few of the men. As I went down a slight grade an unusual sight greeted my eyes. There in full priestly regalia stood a man of the cloth in front of a table, which held the high sacraments, blessing soldiers as they bent on their knees in front of him. What was unusual about this scene was that artillery shells were whistling overhead. The priest was standing as erect as an arrow; the men were probably glad that they were on their knees in case a shell exploded right there.

I sat down close by to watch, but not too far from a foxhole into which I could submerge if the occasion called for it; hypnotized by this religious exercise, I just sat and watched Catholic boys coming over the hill to kneel in front of the priest to be blessed and possibly get killed in the process, not to speak of the priest who in my opinion was taking an unnecessary chance with his life. As fast as the soldiers were blessed, they moved right along back to their units .

I was startled out of my trance by a voice from the rear calling out my name. Turning I saw it was Jim Barry, who was later killed in action, out of M company and Boston. What's going on? I asked. He muttered back something about a Catholic holiday that came in February, in which Catholics were blessed by a priest. Grabbing me by the arm, he yelled over the whistles and noise of the exploding shells, "Come along and get your throat blessed."

"But I'm a Jew," I answered.

"I know," he replied.

"This is for everyone. One's religion does not stand in the way. The priest blesses everyone."

Listening to his logical reasons I was almost tempted to go, especially the way he tugged at my arm. Then I thought, it was all right for him to go because he was a Catholic, but what if God got mad at me for turning to another religion? He had been good to me. I hadn't been hit yet after eight months of combat—only a case of malaria. I was still alive. Suppose God got mad at me and ended my life or took away my arms or legs? Reluctantly, I told Jim to go ahead without me.

My curiosity had been satisfied. Then I went back to my former position to keep an eye on the road. I ran into another soldier who told me the regimental colonel had been relieved and a Colonel Darby had taken command of the regiment. Colonel Darby had commanded the three battalions of rangers that had walked into a trap set by the Germans and had been captured or destroyed.

This soldier named Smith, who was in the communication section and sometimes was on the switchboard, told me of a conversation between the Battalion Commander Tryon (who later was badly wounded) and Colonel Darby. Colonel Tyron was in a depressed mood, so when Colonel Darby called and told him to snap out of it, Colonel Tryon told him he had lost over half of his battalion. Colonel

Darby answered, "Don't feel bad; I lost almost three battalions and I'm still able to command! *C'est le guerre!*"

The next week was the deciding factor; the troops held and stopped the Germans. Then the battle went back to an almost typical World War I scenario.

Our battalion was reorganized and moved out to reinforce the other two battalions of the regiment that were still on the line. Moving up, we had to move along the British 1st Division line. Our platoon moved cautiously but swiftly in the daylight hours. This was a mistake; the enemy spotted us moving along the road. A barrage of enemy shells started falling in the immediate area. At the first sound of the whistles, I looked for a depression in the ground, or a foxhole, whichever came first. Seeing a deep shell hole a few yards to my right and with a burst of speed that would have made any Olympic sprinter proud, I reached the shell hole and jumped in, almost falling on one of two occupants who were British soldiers. The first words out of those men were, "Are you Commandos?" This was the second time that reference had been made to me. Those guys must be nuts to think that I even looked like a commando, but as I later thought about it, we were running wildly out in the open along their flank and closer to the enemy lines, while bullets and artillery shells were going off all around us.

"No," I answered, as I made myself comfortable in their hole, handing over a package of Camels which they accepted with thanks.

I noticed one of them had been reading a letter.

"Don't let me interrupt you reading your mail," I said.

His reply was, "It's from my wife. She says I've just become a father."

"Congratulations," were my next words, where upon he angrily said he hadn't been home in two years. "Those goddam Yanks," then looking up at me and in an apologetic voice he said "I don't mean you Yanks here. Those Yanks in London."

I told him I understood what he was saying. The poor bastard had a wife who had the nerve to tell him that she had been sleeping with other men. How stupid can you be?

After offering them a couple more cigarettes, we took off and left their shell hole. They looked at us as if we were some kind of heroes; yet we were the same as they were, just plain ordinary infantrymen. We weren't even in a rifle company, like they were, but our seeming lack of fright and tendency to move around seemed to impress them. What they didn't know was that we were just as scared as they were. I often wondered if they ever got home and if the soldier saw his wife, or had he gotten killed and saved his wife a lot of trouble.

As we moved to our new position down the road, bren-gun carriers (a gas-operated machine gun that was carried on an armored vehicle about the size of a jeep) ran up and down the road, firing their machine guns into the Germans alongside the road, while German tanks and artillery fired almost point blank at these British mosquito-like vehicles that contained men of indescribable bravery. As we moved further up the road tanks hiding behind us almost destroyed farmhouses. They were firing point blank at advancing German troops. Moving swiftly along the road, we could see some of our tanks burning from direct hits; no survivors were running from these tanks. What a scene! Everyone was being shot at or destroyed; yet, this scene overcame any fear that I felt at that time. What was to come later could best be explained as if one had a constant toothache—one got used to it. It hurt, but the daily pain was expected. So it was with the fear! It was there all the time.

Things started to settle down a bit after this last attack, and I dug into the ground that night and was glad to get a night's sleep. Early in the morning I was awakened by my roommate whispering in my ear to take a look out on the road. All was quiet; it was like being in a park back home on a Sunday where one could only hear the birds. There almost alongside my hole walked two medics with their helmets pulled down on their heads and Red Cross flags in their hands. In back of them walked General Eagles. In back of him came jeeps and ambulances. They were advancing toward the enemy lines. Not even a rifle shot could be heard; we soon got the word that a truce had been declared just long enough for the dead and wounded from both sides to be picked up on the battlefield. My God, the general had a lot of guts; I wouldn't have exposed myself to those German bastards, even with a truce. I was so shaken from the previous day's battles that I didn't want to get out of my hole.

Strange as it seems, quiet reigned over the battlefield as those wounded and dying were moved back to our lines. The carnage on both sides can only be recorded as indescribable. The day passed swiftly and with it the truce. As the last ambulances moved quietly to the rear with their dead and wounded, the beachhead came alive with artillery fire. All that one could do was thank God for the few hours of the truce.

It seemed that after the truce ended the bombardment wasn't as severe as it had been previously. The enemy had to replenish their ammunition dumps, so we could almost voluntarily come out of our holes. Our platoon set up the battalion CP in an open field and, taking advantage of the lull in the fighting, everyone started walking around with abandon, until the Germans started throwing in an artillery barrage. Running for the nearest foxhole, I found myself racing along side a yellow snake that seemed to be about five or six feet long. He seemed to be heading in the same direction as I was and going as fast as I was. Of course, I could have tried to take him out with a few shots from my M-1, but who had time to fire a gun while running for a foxhole? Looking down to see if the snake was still there, I had seemed to have forgotten why I was running at such a great speed. Sure enough, the snake was gliding along at an incredible speed; could he be as scared of the breaking artillery shells as I was? There we were, the snake and I in a race which would have been most comical to any onlooker, and funny enough to have made Charlie Chaplin look like a straight man, but it wasn't funny to me.

As the shells came in faster, the snake and I moved faster, both headed for the nearest foxhole, which we both reached in a dead heat. Not wishing to challenge it for the safety of the foxhole, I overran it as the snake glided easily into the entrance. Hitting the ground, while the shells burst all around me, I found out one thing. I had always thought that there was nothing I could be more scared of than artillery fire, but now it was sharing a foxhole with a snake. This area of Anzio had been very swampy and had been noted for its malaria bearing mosquitoes. Maybe it was also a habitat for snakes which had been blasted out of their holes in the ground by the tons of high explosives that had been expended on the beachhead.

After this incident, I dug a hole into higher ground near a roadway where jeeps from the rear with supplies traversed daily. Their dust during daylight hours brought down German artillery barrages constantly; finally, almost all traffic was consigned to the darker hours of each day.

The Germans weren't through. They tried one more offensive and during this battle laid down the most murderous artillery barrages imaginable. It was a wonder that more soldiers didn't have their senses leave them; it was during one of these barrages that our platoon lieutenant, who had been with the company since December, and had replaced the lieutenant from South Carolina and had been wounded at Venafro, came crawling by my hole crying like a bride at a church whose groom failed to make an appearance. He apparently didn't even know that there was a foxhole there; it was so well camouflaged. He was a nice guy, a former Irish policeman from New York, but this was one place where bombs, artillery shells, and bullets could break down the strongest minds. He wasn't the only one weeping, Rerter was right behind him as they both made their way to the rear. Where they were going I didn't know, but I never mentioned the weeping scene to anyone. Both those men were to be shortly extracted from the beachhead as battle-fatigue cases.

The battalion was relieved and brought back to what was called a rest area. One day while back there some of the men from the regiment were lined up with whitish tags; among them were Rerter and the other soldier who kept complaining because his name didn't end in "y" and thus he wouldn't have been there. All of these men had been tagged as psychos and were to be shipped off the beachhead, back to Naples, and reassigned to a unit in the rear. How lucky could one get? How did they get picked? Word had come down, most likely to the company commanders, to get rid of those soldiers who had shown the most fear and had broken under combat. I was just as scared as they were but had never shown the emotion coupled with tears to put me in their category.

When I found out why they were being shipped back, I almost made them sorry that they were going back. Some of these men were the kind who tried to impress everyone with their manliness and now it was their turn to take the jibes and taunts that I thought they so richly deserved. They must have been glad when the order came for them to move out, just to get away from my jeers. After all, some of these men who were noncoms had tried to show a superior masculinity from the time they were still in the States and I was only trying to make them feel as if they were like beaten dogs, retreating with their tails between their legs.

Replacements came into the company and we got a new platoon lieutenant named Trow and, my luck, he had to be Jewish. The battalion also received a new battalion commander named Weber, a West Pointer. These were the worst type, because they were gung-ho, aggressive, and especially, when they were new to combat, a person like this could be dangerous to his own men. Because Anzio had now developed to a static battlefield, he could demand things of his own men that were most irrational.

When the battalion moved back up to the front and he was settled in his CP, the stench of the dead cattle that had been killed by previous artillery fire and didn't seem to be much of an annoyance to other commanders, became an obsession with Colonel Weber.

He sent out an order to bury the cattle immediately; it wouldn't have been too hard to comply with if it had been in another area off the beachhead, but he wanted them buried where the shells were dropping without letup and during the middle of the day when the enemy could spot anyone walking around. It was a most insane order and only to relieve the smelling sensibilities of his nose; he didn't care how many men would be killed in this senseless maneuver.

Some of us went out to find and bury the cattle, but all we did was get as far as some abandoned foxholes and waited until dark, then went back to the CP, saying we had buried what cattle we found. The conversation in the foxhole had been filled with the most deleterious profanity concerning the colonel and everyone agreed he could go to hell before we would stand out in the open and bury dead cattle in order to protect him from the decaying odor while exploding artillery shells sprayed their shrapnel all around us.

A few days later, he went out to the line companies and was horrified to find that the men hadn't shaved for days; he left an order with the company commanders that everyone was to shave by the next day when he would be back. If not, he would court-martial anyone needing a shave. Now there was just enough water to drink, let alone shave with; enemy fire was on everyone's mind, not how one's face would look if one would be killed. Back he came the next day, but no one had shaved. His mistake was that everyone would have welcomed a court-martial just to get out of the line. He had to eat his words and started to learn the hard way how one treats the troops on the front line because there's no punishment like waiting to be killed. He seemed to think he could push the Germans back by himself. He soon became an anathema to many of those who had to suffer his idiosyncrasies. Luckily my contact with him was minimal.

One of the jobs of our platoon was to lay barbed wire, something we had practiced back in the States, so when the battlelines got a little static we were called upon to do this job. Out we went from the forward battalion CP and through our own lines where we could smell the dead bodies of our own men who hadn't been picked up by the graves registration section. Who could blame them? The enemy fire was so intense that it would have been almost suicidal to attempt it.

The job was aided by the enemy flares that lit up the night skies, making the front look like a night game at Yankee Stadium. As soon as the flares died down we would immediately get up from our prone positions and continue to lay the wire.

One night coning back from laying wire, a few German planes

flew overhead and started dropping their personal bombs. Caught out in the open, there was nothing to do but hit the ground and pray as the shrapnel burst and sprayed over our heads.

Just as soon as that attack was ending, we all got up and started moving out fast when one of the soldiers started crying and having tantrums. It was Sergeant Beery; he was the one who had taken my place when I was busted back in the States. Some noncom—I never saw him again after that night as he had gone to the medics and been removed from the beachhead. However, my ordeal wasn't over, for one of the men with us was hit and I was relegated to stay with him until the others could send the medics back with a stretcher to bring him to the first aid station. While waiting, the Germans raked over that part of the front with their nightly artillery barrage. Lowering the injured soldier into an abandoned dugout, I got into the hole after him to sweat out the barrage while waiting for the medics; it was most unnerving. After ten minutes which seemed like ten hours, it let up. After about an hour, the medics showed up and put the GI on a stretcher. I didn't even know his name; he had been a replacement and had only been in the company a few days. I don't know whether he had been faking his injury. In the dark, it's hard to tell and you bandage a guy up if he points to the injury.

The action had slowed, the planes had gone home, and except for an occasional flare lighting up the sky, it was as serene as one could expect. Machine guns rattling in the distance had a nice easy sound, unlike an artillery shell breaking over our heads. Then we all started off. The medics were carrying the hurt GI in their stretcher. Taking my time, I let them get ahead of me as I presumed an ambulance would be waiting once they got to the road. All of a sudden another artillery barrage started; I headed for the first empty dugout. The medics had disappeared; probably they dove into another hole or maybe they had gotten to the road. I wasn't far from it, but I stayed in the hole as the Germans pounded the area with a tremendous barrage. If they had known those holes were empty and they were wasting their ammunition, the barrage would have come to a quick halt.

Meanwhile, they almost shook my teeth loose. My mind was already loose, so I thought I would defy them. Lighting up a cigarette and trying to relax succeeded for a while. Then the barrage seemed to be moving away from where I was. It was a sweeping barrage and the enemy was going to catch as many of their enemy as possible. As the line of fire moved away, I thought I would make a dash for the road and then up to the CP where we were dug in.

I reached the road and started to run toward the farm complex when all of a sudden, shells started hitting the towers and exploding on the area. The towers must have consisted of about four to six feet of solid stone. I was startled. Should I continue running and try to make our position or look for an abandoned foxhole alongside the road? There wasn't any time to look as exploding shells started to hit the roadway only about 40 yards ahead of me. The only thing left was to hit the ground. Lying on that open road while the shell fire crept up and down alongside the road was enough to put fear into the devil himself; the road shook from the explosions, but I lay there not daring to get up for fear that the shrapnel might cut me in half. After what seemed like hours to me, but probably was no more than five or ten minutes, the artillery barrage stopped. Knowing that the Germans could start shelling again within minutes, I started to get up. A strange thing occurred that had never happened to me before. My legs seemed to be immobilized. They wouldn't move. My mind was clear, but I couldn't make my body get up out of the road. What the hell was this? I hadn't been hit with any shrapnel. Lying on an open road waiting for an artillery barrage to begin wasn't my style. Try as I could, my legs just wouldn't move. What a situation to be in. For a person who had been most adept at finding the slightest depression on any landscape where I might be traveling, I couldn't even get up off the road to look for some protection against the barrage that I knew would be coming at any time.

Something had to be the matter with me. Ten minutes must have gone by and my body was still immobile. My mind was alert, but the rest of my body acted as if it was frozen in time. Slowly my arms came back to my command and were able to lift my body up to a foot or more above the road so I could see any shallow spots along the roadside where I could drag my body for protection whether the shelling started in again or not.

One minute I was crawling; then suddenly my legs came into action and my body was moving at an almost indescribable pace. I rushed toward the stone towers that a few minutes earlier had been the target of a number of shells. I told my story to a few of the fellows. They told me to go into the battalion medics, figuring that the doctor would give me something to relieve my mind. I told the doctor my story. He said, "You need a rest; the tension has been too much." Thinking he was going to send me back to the rear or maybe back to Naples, my spirits picked up. "We'll be getting relieved in a few days," he said, "and then you'll be able to get the rest you need."

Sure enough, orders came through the next day that our battalion was to be relieved the following day. It gave everyone a chance to get halfway back to normal for the four days we were back. It was only a couple of miles, and the rest area was situated in a wooded area which was susceptible to artillery fire. Every company was given a certain section, so some soldiers were sent back in the daylight hours so they could direct their companies to their area and the dugouts the men would occupy. I was one of those picked to go back with another soldier named Chucky Balter.

Walking back to the area was no mean feat. Every inch of the beachhead was under observation by the enemy and smoke pots hadn't been in use that close to the front at this time. Smoke pots were being used mostly in the port area to protect the supplies doming in off LSTs. Though it was dangerous to be walking in this area, it was back enough to be out of range of the machine guns that would crackle almost incessantly all night long.

The biggest danger was the shells that the Nazis would drop all over the beachhead indiscriminately. So instead of using what were called roads, one would walk in the open fields where there were many empty dugouts that once had housed soldiers. However, the lines had moved forward so the only thing left in the dugouts were unused packages of cigarettes, sometimes cartons of Fleetwood, Old Gold, Pall-Mall and other brands that weren't too popular with the troops. Camels, Luckys, and Chesterfields were the most popular; one never found those brands in abandoned dugouts.

Companies usually were either at half- or three-quarter strength most of the time, but experienced mess sergeants ordered their supplies as if their companies were at full strength of around two hundred men. There were always enough rations to go around and more; that's why cigarettes that were unpopular could be cast aside in an evacuated foxhole. As for me, if Camels weren't in evidence, I would reluctantly settle for a package of Luckys or Chesterfields, but if I was running low, I might grab a package of Old Golds but never a Raleigh.

Chucky Balter and I warily made our way back to a wooded area that was used for a rest area for the troops coming off the line. It was about two miles from the front and seemed like a miniature forest with dugouts already in place where the men could wash and try to shave in relatively peace and quiet for a few minutes as artillery shells passed overhead headed for the troops assigned to the area of the port.

The battalions were relieved at night as it was too dangerous to move so many men around in daylight hours, and as each company came into the so-called rest area, the two men who had been designated to show each platoon its area had to be on the alert and immediately show the men to their dugouts as it was too dangerous for so many men too bunch up in such a small area.

When Chucky and I got to the rest area, we made contact with the men from the battalion and they showed us where our company was to be quartered and where each platoon was to be located. We in turn were to wait in the dark at the edge of the woods and show our company's men where to find their dugouts. There were lines of white tape and string strung along the pathways to make it easier to locate our rest area in the dark woods. After having been shown the designated areas for the company, Chucky and I went back to the roadway where the battalion would be coming down to enter the wooded area.

As I approached the roadway, there was Jim Barry standing talking to about six other scouts from the other companies in the battalion, so we went over and joined them for cigarettes and conversation. The conversation went from how the Russians were doing on the Eastern Front to what was going on at Cassino, and to what rumors were going around that the division might be relieved and sent to England for the invasion of France. I had known Jim Barry for quite a while; he was with M Company, a heavy weapons company. The other fellows were scouts from L, K, and I Companies and had been around quite a while in the battalion. I had always gone over to see them when we got to a rest area; they were quite intelligent and a lively discussion was had by all when we got together.

As the darkness of this rainy day drew toward early evening, the Germans started throwing artillery shells all over the area that was supposed to be a rest area. One would have thought that they had advance knowledge that the battalions were being rotated at that time because the shells came crashing into this area as if there was a Kraut artillery observer sitting in one of the trees. They had misjudged the time of our battalions arrival by about ten minutes, but I had to wait at the edge of the woods as my company could be coming along at any minute. Jim Barry and the other scouts took off to where their companies' areas were located.

As I lay on the ground with my fingers literally trying to dig further into the earth as all hell broke loose in this compacted area, loud screams for help burst forth farther into the wooded area. The cries seemed to be coming from all directions. It wasn't unusual to me; how many times those piercing cries of dying soldiers had pierced my ears, but what could I do? Should I get up and be killed or lay in that position and be blown to bits anyway? It's a wonder my mind didn't explode with the shells.

As I lay with my head practically stuck in the ground, I was almost sure I heard someone calling my name, but should I get up and look around in the darkness? Better to lie there than to go wildly off into the darkness looking for whoever was calling me, but the voice almost had a familiar ring, something like Jim Barry's Bostonian twang. It came out of the darkness one or two more times; then all was silent. Even the artillery fire slowed up, luckily for the troops had started coming into the area. I was up on my feet looking for my company and after finding them I tried to show them to the dugouts in their area before the bastard Nazis started shelling again.

It wasn't until close to midnight before the troops were settled down. Then I couldn't find the dugout that Chucky Balter and I had picked out. What a frustrating experience! Soaked to the skin and worn down by the nerve-wracking shell fire, and in utter desperation, I was ready to lie down on the soaked ground. Luckily, we stumbled upon the dugout. It wasn't as if it had six-foot walls and ceilings of solid rock, but it was a sanctuary. Out on the field any hole in the ground became almost the equivalent of a castle. This dugout was only about 5 feet into the earth but it had been built like a rotunda. Half was sticking out of the ground but the roof was solid and the earth where we had laid a blanket had turned to mud. The water from the constant rain had seeped into our enlarged and covered foxhole.

I laid down on the soaked blanket. It wasn't an unusual situation, but when one comes back to what is considered a rest area, one expects better accommodations. I awoke from my sleep by the sound of whining coming from outside the dugout. Looking out, I saw a form lying directly in the doorway. Asking who the hell it was in no polite tongue, a voice answered, "DeForest."

"What the hell do you want? And what are you doing lying out in the rain exposed to shell fire?"

His answer was that he had no one to hole up with and was left to shift for himself. I told him to come inside; he didn't even have a blanket to lay on. I told him he could stay until morning and then would have to find another hole. He was a replacement in the company like Balter was. Sometimes these replacements acted as if they were helpless, but there might have been good reason.

Laying back on my blanket, I lit up a cigarette. I took slow puffs while reflecting on the events of the evening. The other two had fallen asleep almost instantly, and then DeForest started to snore most violently. (Later I learned that two of the fellows he had shared a dugout with had thrown him out because of his snoring and that explained why he had appeared on my doorstep).

As I lay there pondering the events of the evening, my thoughts kept going back to that voice that seemed to keep calling what sounded like "Gersh, Gersh." Maybe it was my imagination. However, how the hell were the Germans able to lay in such an artillery barrage at almost the exact time that the troops were to be moving back to this rest area? Had the Nazis infiltrated our lines with a few men laying unnoticed in the background directing the shelling of the woods by radio? I started to doze off. After putting the remains of the cigarette in the mud, my eyes closed.

The next morning when we awoke the sun was shining. The morning was just the opposite of the previous evening; it was almost springlike though it was still winter. Someone yelled out that breakfast was being served. We went down a trail and in a little clearing our company kitchen was set up and hot coffee was being served out of the garbage cans that were sometimes used for pots. What a welcome sight! There were hot pancakes, too. Our mess sergeant, John, was really on the ball. By afternoon there was a mail call and some letters and newspapers were handed to me. My time would be occupied for a while, but my greatest interest was the news, and that would come from the BBC.

Everyone was more at ease this morning; later, I found out Jim Barry had been killed with four of the other men that I had been talking to the previous evening. So with a glance at a month-old newspaper, I tried to wipe this painful incident from my mind as I had done with others in the past. However, Jim Barry had received a thirty-day leave for home and rather than wait for his leave to come back in Naples where his company commander wanted him to go, he wanted to stay with his company on Anzio until it came through. He felt guilty about leaving while others were still in combat. What a nice guy, but what a horrendous mistake.

That afternoon, with nothing to do but relax in my home in the woods, suddenly it became a nightmare. Balter kept whimpering about a wife and kid back in Pennsylvania and how he would never get to see them again. His lament turned to tears and was quite upsetting, especially after the events of the previous evening. This guy wasn't someone for me to be sharing a dugout with. Things were bad enough. Who wanted to listen to someone's teary stories of home and how he had to get there—a most depressing situation. As he wore glasses, I told him to throw them away and then to go down to the medics and tell them he lost his glasses and couldn't see. I never thought he could get away with it, but I wanted to get him away from me for a while and go aggravate someone else.

The next morning he went down to the medics with his story. About an hour later he came back to the dugout, with a tag hanging from his jacket; it was his ticket off the beachhead. He was being shipped out as if he had been badly wounded. What I had told him as a joke had turned out to be a gift from heaven. He picked up everything that belonged to him. He could see pretty well as he walked through the mud back to where the sick and wounded were to be evacuated. I couldn't believe my eyes and ears; the doctor didn't even know that he wore glasses. He left without even a thank you.

All day I brooded. How did this happen? Here my wheeze had been getting worse and when running hard, especially under shell fire it was hard to catch my breath. I remembered when I was back in the hospital in Tunis. After an exam the doctor had asked me if I had trouble breathing, and like a fool I said no. I figured my shortness of breath came from my cigarette smoking. My God, if Balter could get a free ride out of this hell, it was worth a try! It wasn't like a month earlier, when one of the men told me to say I had an ulcer like he claimed he got off the beachhead, but I was too honest for that. But now this wheezing was legitimate, so down to the medics I went. After an examination, the doctor told me that it was bronchial asthma. "Stay out of wet and damp places," he said. I told him my dugout was half mud, and asked what am I supposed to do. He told me there was nothing he could do for me. He'd just gotten orders from corps that no one was to leave the beach unless they had lost an arm or a leg. Balter was lucky he had gone in the day before the order had come.

It was a good try! How the hell did I get into this? It seemed as if everyone in the company had gone down to the medics when I told them how easily Balter had gotten out of the outfit.

I went over to battalion headquarters to pick up some papers and talked to Petit, who was on duty. He had a piece of paper in his hand; it listed men of the battalion who were killed or missing in action. Felix Subvervi's name was on the list as missing. Petit was laughing, "Subvervi got captured; he was broken down to a private. He won't be collecting corporal's pay," he continued to laugh. Looking at him peculiarly I walked away.

The next morning when I went down to eat breakfast, everyone was talking about the CP being hit with a direct hit by an artillery shell. Petit was killed and the lieutenant occupying the CP was badly wounded. I wondered if Petit's laughing at Subervi's misfortune could have had anything to do with the incident. Could it be an omen from God that war is no laughing matter? I never laughed at another soldier's (on our side) bad luck after that.

The four days in the rear soon passed and we went back up to the lines with nothing unusual happening—if one likes to think of constant artillery shells whistling overhead and the whistle of bombs coming down from the sky every night as inconsequential.

We got a new battalion commander, a Lieutenant Colonel Webber. Tryon had been badly wounded. Webber was a West Pointer and he always liked to give it the old college try and this attitude was anathema to the rest of us; it was bad enough standing up to the enemy fire. Who needed a junior Napoleon looking over our shoulders?

Again our battalion was sent back for a four-day rest, not to the woods but another area of the beach about a mile away. It was more open, but now our forces had started to use smoke, a sort of fog that was carried in some sort of cans. I knew little about their operation: it probably was put into use by the beach engineers. This smoke or fog would be released from containers and would immediately go skyward and like a curtain going up instead of down would block out the visible goings-on at the beach or its immediate environs; thus, making it almost safe to walk around in a rear area, as the enemy wasn't able to see any of the activity going on. Of course, they still lobbed in artillery shells and many places had been zeroed in, such as crossroads or important areas where supplies or ammunition had been stored, so whether targets were visible or not, indiscriminate shelling continued, taking its daily toll of those unlucky enough to be in areas that were under constant shelling day or night. It wasn't unusual to see our ammunition dumps hit every night and the exploding shells would light up the sky as if it was the Fourth of July. One of these shells going overhead every night sounded like a freight train and was fired from a railway gun that was hidden in a tunnel during the day. Its noise wasn't so discernible at the front as there were so many artillery shells exploding around our positions, but as one went further to the rear the noise from this gun, called the Anzio Express, was quite audible as it streaked its way to the beach 4 or 5 miles to the rear; it was one of the few times I felt sorry for rear echelon troops.

Showers had been set up for all troops that were in a rest area and so our company's turn came to take a shower. It was almost two months since I had showered, but when the 1st sergeant told me to get into a truck to go to the showers, I balked. Others got on the truck and left; I stood there refusing the sergeant's order. "Do you think I'm going to stand naked far from a hole to jump in while the Germans shell the area?" I asked. "I'd rather stay dirty." Frisbee was upset; he called me filthy and demanded I take a shower. "Besides. . . it was healthy." I answered back it was more healthy to keep away from German shell fire if possible and to stay fully clothed; I was damned if I was going to get killed taking a shower.

The next day Frisbee approached me again, and asked me about a shower. This time I softened up and told him I would go with the next load from the battalion. Getting on the truck and riding to the destination was most difficult. The phobia of having a shell explode on or near the truck without being able to take cover in the fields was enough to scare hell out of anyone. It was like being a caged animal waiting to be shot. Arriving at the showers, I couldn't wait to jump off the truck. A short line was waiting to enter the showers, which were almost completely in the open except for a small piece of canvas that was set up like a wall to face in the direction of the enemy. The smoke pots were going at full blast and as the curtain of fog that was generated by the smoke pots hung in the afternoon air obliterating any view of the activities going on, I gained new confidence as I took my place in the line and took off clothing piece by piece as the line edged toward the shower. Just as I removed my socks, spray from the showers started to cover my head.

"Next," a voice shouted out and before the voice could be raised again, I was under the shower, which was one of six that had been placed there so the men could move through faster. I used my own soap. Soap was passed out there, but who wanted to use the remains of someone else's soap? My body was soon lathered and for the next five minutes I forgot where I was and enjoyed the warm waters that poured over my body.

"Let's go," a voice shouted. My turn was over; fresh socks, pants, and a shirt were handed out. There were only two sizes: small and large, but my problem wasn't over. I was allergic to wool, and there wasn't any shirt that didn't have some wool. Pants weren't such a problem. However. I was able to get a fatigue shirt that was worn by the troops when they were in a rest area or were doing some dirty work in the rear.

Walking down a gully, where other men from my battalion were waiting for a truck, a bit of nervousness came back to me. How long would it be before our transportation came for us? I didn't relish this area which was bereft or any dugouts or places to hide if enemy shelling started. Finally, our truck arrived and the ride back to our area continued without any incident, so when I jumped off the truck any nervousness that I had when the trip started was completely gone.

That night even though there was another day left for our rest period, a section of our platoon was sent up to the lines that night to dig a dugout for the forward battalion CP. It was a new sector and that was part of our job. When we arrived at our destination, we found that we were to dig the command post into a bank of a road that rested about 25 yards from the enemy. There were no foxholes or dugouts close by where we were digging. The only place where there was any kind of protection was under a little bridge, about 10 yards long. It connected the roads along the embankments, and that's where everyone ran when enemy shells started falling on our side of the road. The first time everyone made it safe to this emergency shelter, but no one wanted to leave when the shelling stopped. Hook, who was in charge, started to chastise the men in order to get them back to finishing the job. Poor Al, he had a tough job. No one wanted to go. Finally we went back to complete the job. The dugout was almost finished when the shelling started again. Everyone ran for the under pass; only this time one of the men got there a little late—about 2 seconds late. He was hit with shrapnel. Dick Long, poor guy had gotten a slow start. The call went out for medics.

It was only a few minutes and the medics came. They bandaged Dick up, gave him a shot to knock him out, put him on a stretcher and carried him a little closer to what was called a road, but still left him laying next to the embankment, as a jeep would have to come to pick him up to bring him to the hospital. The medics had to go back to the line company that was just in front of us, and we had to go back to finish our job. Poor Dick, he was left practically alone. About 20 minutes later we came back to that spot. Long was still laying there. My God, no one had come for him yet. He was sleeping contentedly when shells started dropping again. Everyone made for a few foxholes that had been dug by another unit and then abandoned as the lines moved a little forward. Everyone got safely into those holes and as I looked out, there was Long still asleep on the stretcher waiting to be moved. We couldn't even move him to our holes. If he had ever known what was going on, he would have died of fright, but he was lucky. Though shrapnel was flying all around he didn't get hit again and survived to be put on a jeep that was being used to bring the wounded to the hospital.

The next day our unit moved up to the positions where we had been busy digging out new dugouts. The colonel had gone out to look over the rest of the battalion, and as he went from company to company he was reported to have gotten more irritated; he couldn't understand why the men didn't shave every day. He gave specific orders that when he came back the next day they had better be shaved. What a laugh! Colonel Weber from West Point didn't know what it was like in actual combat and thought he was spewing out orders to his rear echelon command. I heard the men laughed at him. His threat of a court-martial was taken as a dare by the men. What a break is what many of them thought. What a way to get out of the lines and stay from enemy firepower. It was hard enough to keep the line companies in drinking water, never mind having enough water to shave with every day, Weber never carried out his threat; he knew better. That's what happens when a gung-ho-know-nothing-West-Pointer who doesn't want to learn, takes command of a battalion, but his foolishness kept everyone in the battalion on their toes, especially those closest to him, such as the soldiers in my company. I was to be a recipient of his idiocy about a month later.

As we lay in our positions alongside of the road embankment, time seemed to stand still. Every night the mess sergeant came up with rations, and the mail plus the army papers such as *Stars & Stripes* and when one got a chance to read it, the information that the paper carried was surprisingly good.

One day a notice came down to the company that there would be Passover Services held at the hospital and a truck would be waiting at the end of the road for all those of the Jewish faith wanting to attend. How time had flown, but attending became a problem. Was it worth the while to get out of this position which was almost constantly under artillery fire and take a chance getting on a truck and have a shell explode alongside or in the truck? I couldn't show the other men that I was Godless, and besides they said there would be matzoh and wine served, but that hospital was always under artillery and bombing attacks. I decided to go. What the hell; I was jumping from the frying pan to the fire or maybe it was the other way around. The next morning I started the walk to the road where the truck would be waiting, not wanting to go to the crossroad which was zeroed in by the enemy. A shell would drop there about every two minutes and anyone not timing their crossing of that area was in trouble. So I cut across an open field in a light trot, and half bent over, ready to hit the ground at the slightest sound of a whistle. In fact I moved along pretty fast until the truck came into sight sitting in a depressed part of the road and slightly shielded from any shrapnel that might be flying around from exploding shells. I approached the truck. A familiar face appeared; it was Leo Penn. Patting me on the back, he said, "I knew you'd show up." Penn was with the antitank platoon. Though we were in the same company, our platoons were positioned in different areas, so sometimes we didn't see each another for weeks at a time.

Jumping into the truck with Penn, a few of the other fellows were slightly familiar, but most were unknown to me. The truck started up and moved slowly forward as we all sat in a tense position, waiting uneagerly for an artillery attack or at the last for a strafing attack by a lone plane seeing a lone truck on the road.

In a few minutes another truck appeared and it was full of soldiers heading in the same direction. After a tense and bumpy ride the truck arrived at the entrance to the hospital. Jumping off, the men wasted no time heading for the tents that were part of the hospital compound. Standing at one entrance was a doctor who directed all those who came for the services to where they were to assemble. I went to a tent and saw benches spread out; the tent covered a partly dug-out piece of ground that was about three feet deep. It was a little protection against flying shrapnel though the area was dug below the ground. It was very wide and the canvas tent offered little protection. How could anyone laying in a hospital tent remain calm under such circumstances? When I came into the entrance here were nurses standing by their dugouts which seemed to be well dug in, and with sandbags covering the entrances and the sides of their dugouts. That would have been the place to hold the services, but how do you get that many men in one of those dugouts?

The services were started and I think a chaplain conducted them, but I was so nervous being in such an exposed area, I didn't know whether it was a chaplain or the doctor who had greeted us at the entrance. Matzoh and wine were passed out; my appetite was gone—this was no place to dally, but I couldn't leave until the services were ended. The hospital in normal combat conditions would have been a wonderful place to relax, but stories had run loose how dangerous it was at this medical reception area. If I told any one that I wanted to get back to my hole at the front, that person would have thought I was insane. As the service continued, it became apparent to me how many Jews were attached to infantry companies. Normally I would have lingered and got into a conversation, but I guess my social life had gone begging for the past two months or so. Or maybe I was getting psychotic—funny the services didn't seem to mean too much to me. Everyone was living day to day and one was resigned to the fate that was thrown upon everyone's head that was on the beachhead. What the hell was the matter with me? I usually took everything with a grain of salt—even being scared to death.

Leo Penn was full of pep; one wouldn't know he would be going back to the front in a few minutes. Lighting up a cigarette we got into a sort of satirical conversation about how lucky we were to be at such a lovely resort town in Italy in the middle of a war while in the European Theater most Americans were stuck in fog-shrouded England. So ended another day at Anzio as everyone started to get into the trucks that had arrived to take us back up on the lines.

It wasn't long after my journey back to the hospital for the

Passover Services that an order came down that our division was to be relieved and we were going back to the rear for a rest. But where the hell could one go on the beachhead and get away from the German artillery? However who cared? One wasn't susceptible to snipers or any kind of bullets. It was welcome news. The rumors had started that the division was to be relieved by the 5th Division which was supposed to be in Alaska. Everyone was in a jubilant mood. Alaska! Why not exchange places with them there? Even the North Pole would have been acceptable.

We moved out one company at a time. As one company moved out the outfit that was relieving us would move in. In the early morning darkness the men moved silently across the abandoned fields that were filled with empty dugouts, a quick escape to safety as we hastily moved to the rear hoping that "Axis Sally" wouldn't be broadcasting our departure, as her fellow Nazis would be throwing artillery shells all over the landscape as we headed for our rest area. The Germans had a habit of knowing when the troops were being relieved.

After walking about two miles, we reached the bivouac area where trucks were waiting to take the men to the rest area that was to be our home for the next two weeks. Gazing at the truck area, the soldiers quietly jumped up into the trucks and silence was a prerequisite, as everyone knew. If one wasn't present at this movement, one wouldn't know that even one soldier was being transported out of this area. Everyone knew that his life depended on his silence and as the trucks moved out of the bivouac area the only noise was the purring of the motors.

As the trucks continued along the road, there were occasional flashes of light; these were the enemy shells lighting the beachhead area. The rear echelon troops were finding out what war was all about at Anzio. Night attacks by the German air force and the constant artillery fire thrown by the Nazis forced those who, until Anzio, had been out of harm's way most of the time, to dig in and pray.

The trucks finally stopped and everyone jumped out of the

trucks and were led into an area that seemed to be covered with trees. Each company was assigned to a different area of this semi-forest. A dugout was pointed out to me. It was to be my home for the next two weeks. Without hesitating I quickly entered my new domicile and lit up a cigarette. What a relief!, Now I could slumber or whatever for a couple of weeks, or so I thought.

Later that afternoon, I was awakened by a call for supper. Slowly I got up and half crawled out of the dugout; everyone seemed to be in a relaxed mood. No shells were bursting in our area; there wasn't any swoosh over our heads which usually signaled shells going over. My God! It was almost paradise. As the men waited in line to walk by the mess crew everyone started to engage in conversation and the only subject was how good it was to be sort of relaxing for a while. So the first day slipped away as the shower area was pointed out. Even mail was distributed that first day of rest; card games weren't long in getting started, but I just wanted to eat my supper, have a smoke, and read whatever papers were on hand, from the *Stars & Stripes* to my local paper, the *Day*, which had become a backlog of twelve or fourteen. Sometimes they were distributed in bunches, mostly in rest areas. How was one to read so many newspapers at the front crouched in a small dugout?

The next morning as I was standing in line for breakfast the 1st sergeant came over to me and said he had a job for me to do. Outraged, I told him this was a rest area; we were supposed to take it easy. He told me to quiet down and listen. "Of course, if you would rather stand guard duty or be at the beckon and call of some clean-up detail, forget it," he said. "I'm going to put you in charge of a water detail. Every day you will take a truck and go for water filling up the five-gallon cans that every company will give you. There will be two men from each company in the battalion that will be assigned to your detail. They will do all the work; you just have to make sure every company gets its full allotment of water every day." That didn't sound too bad; I would be free to do whatever I wanted to after the water was delivered.

That afternoon a driver showed up with ten men on the truck and we took off for the water depot that was located near the town of Anzio about five miles down the road. It was still dangerous driving there, but the dense fog generated by the smoke pots were a welcome curtain to hide behind and the Germans didn't seem to have any reason to fire upon that region as there wasn't anything of consequence in that area. Then as the truck moved along an ammunition dump came into view and almost next to it was the hospital. My God, what a place to put the hospital! As we moved along an oil dump came into sight. It was located on the other side of the hospital. No wonder the hospital was always getting bombed and shelled. The Germans knew the oil and ammunition dumps were there, so they fired upon these installations and hit the hospital every once in a while. Our supply Generals were to blame for the extra casualties in the hospital areas and not entirely those Nazis. As the truck moved along, my eyes still couldn't believe what they saw: those two prerequisites of war, oil and ammunition dumps, straddling a hospital.

I had completely forgotten the danger of traveling on an open road, even in a rear area; the sight of that hospital flanked on both sides by an ammunition and oil dump had left me indignant toward those in charge. I knew that space was at a premium at Anzio but to put wounded soldiers in such an exposed and dangerous position shouldn't even be expected of the dumbest generals.

The truck finally arrived at the water depot and I stood and watched as the men loaded the truck with the 5-gallon cans of water. Walking over to those soldiers who were in charge of this operation, a conversation ensued between us: do you get much shell fire here? How are the air raids was the next question. One of the answers summed up a complete answer to my questions: the Germans haven't forgotten that we are here. After the truck was loaded and we had gotten underway I thought this isn't too bad. I lit up a cigarette as we traveled along. An empty airfield appeared on our right; a few half destroyed planes still lay there. Shell fire had been so intense it had to be abandoned and the fighter planes had to operate from the

Naples area. Our first trip ended uneventful. The water was delivered and I hadn't even taken a deep breath.

After a few days in this rest area, the troops were ordered to stand retreat. One of the few penalties for not being combat troops, but forcing front line men to stand retreat in a rest area that was a target for enemy artillery fire was an order that could only be put out by a lunatic or a West Point General, the kind that seemed to be mostly stationed in Italy.

The regiment was standing retreat on the fourth day in the rest area when the enemy started shelling the area. About six men were killed and twenty or so were wounded, mostly men in the 1st battalion. Those stupid generals back in Naples had done it again, putting men's lives on the line for no reason at all while they enjoyed life back at Naples like Roman centurions, the bastards! At least I didn't have to participate in that foolishness. As far as I knew the retreat formations were cut out after that. I heard the battalion commander say, "Let those bastard generals back in Naples come up and see if we stand retreat."

Every morning I woke up and went for breakfast and the water truck picked me up and all the men were waiting. I felt as if I had my own kingdom. If this could last for the rest of the war, what's a few shells breaking close by? A nice drive to the water depot every day with a nudge to the driver to move faster as we passed the hospital area with the ammo and oil dumps on both sides. I was getting used to an exhilarating life, and what was more amusing, women were never missed or mentioned, and this wasn't even a homosexual society. After supper when everyone went to relax in their own manner, movies were also available. Not being one to assemble in a nonprotected place I stayed away from most social functions. Though the German air force came over the beachhead every night and dropped their bombs, my dugout seemed to me to be the safest place to be, but one evening I decided to go to the movies, against my better judgment. I wasn't disappointed; there was a movie playing with Lena Horne.

With the movie almost half over the German Air Force made an appearance over our sector. We could hear the antiaircraft fire going off. No one ran out of the tent where the movie was being shown; I had looked over the defenses of the tent. It was half dug into the earth with sandbags guarding the sides, not too deep but a little protection against flying shrapnel. Not what I would have wanted but if one wanted to watch Lena Horne, there were a few sacrifices to be made. One was the shrapnel from the personnel bombs that broke apart in mid-air. I was certainly living dangerously; it was the first and last movie I attended. Who wanted to get killed watching a movie? The almost two weeks in the rest area passed by too soon, and I would be joining my regular unit. The lieutenant from S-4 who was in charge of supplies for the battalion asked me to drive his jeep for a week while his driver was enjoying a week's furlough in Naples. It didn't sound bad to me, though I hadn't driven much since I went into the army. Who cared? As long as I didn't have to move up to the front, even just for another week. The first sergeant said it was okay, so when the troops moved back up, I remained a few miles back in the motor pool area. It was a sort of rear echelon, but how rear echelon could it be? Almost parallel to us and a hundred yards away were the tanks of the 1st Armored Division dug into the ground and firing their 90-millimeter guns like artillery pieces. Of course, they received counter battery fire from the Germans, and a few of those shells fell in our area of the motor pool.

The 1st day there, the lieutenant and I dug out an impressive dugout and fortified it with quite a number of sandbags. This dugout was like nothing that I had occupied at the front. There were two bunkbeds in it. The lieutenant had gotten then from supply; he even had a bulb in it. It was attached to the battery in the jeep, and a small radio was hooked up. Imagine listening to Axis Sally every evening, and playing the most popular songs with Bing Crosby. So after digging all day I was tired, but the kitchen was nearby. Eating hot meals three times a day was a luxury that I had to get used to all over again.

Waking up the second morning with practically nothing to do, I couldn't believe my good luck. An occasional shell came over once in a while; it was like being attacked by a mosquito when one was always used to being attacked by stinging bees. Nearby other occupants of the motor pool were shaving. That wasn't anything new, but with electric shavers plugged into the jeep batteries. This was another world, maybe about three miles or so behind the lines. How about those further back? What a life they must lead! Of course on Anzio it was another matter. Even in the rear there were air raid shells exploding and men dying, but in a more leisurely way than at the front.

As I sat smoking while reading the latest edition of *Stars and Stripes*, the lieutenant came over to me and said we had to go back to division supply to pick up a dozen or so Tommy guns as the battalion colonel had wanted them to be delivered up to battalion headquarters that evening. Just my luck, second day in the rear and I had to drive up to the front. I called the battalion commander every name I could think of. What the hell did he want the Tommy guns for? I asked the lieutenant. Something about a raid on the enemy in order to strengthen our lines in L company sector, he answered. Who gives a shit about strengthening the lines, I mumbled to myself as I drove the jeep with the lieutenant toward the division supply dump. Where the hell is it, I asked as I drove to the rear. Let's go to regimental supply first was the answer I got. At regimental supply, we picked up four Tommy guns and so had to continue to division where we finally were able to find another of the guns. Arriving back at our dugout, we had to wait until dark as it would be like committing suicide if we had tried to drive up in the daylight even with the smog from the smoke pots blacking out most of the beachhead. As we got closer to the front, we were more visible and the smoke wasn't laid down on the front for obvious reasons. Any spot of dust arising became a target of enemy artillery. I wasn't enamored with driving up to battalion headquarters. I had walked in that area many times. There were empty dugouts in the fields where one could run to in case of artillery fire, but driving on a road it was hard to hear the whistle of the shells over the noise of the motor and I was afraid I might jump out a second too late. I was getting a little nervous. This was going to he the first time that I had driven a vehicle to the front, though I had walked to the area a few times. As it grew dark the German planes started to come over. They dropped regular bombs and personnel bombs that exploded in midair dropping shrapnel all over the place and giving off a faint light as they exploded. A couple of miles off to the left the Nazis had already started shelling the ammunition dumps. The sky was lit up by the exploding shells; the Germans couldn't miss. So almost every night it looked like the Fourth of July on a grand scale. So with a half moon to light my way, exploding bombs, and bursting shells to aid in giving me light, we were on our way.

Gingerly I drove the jeep in the direction of the front hoping Bed Check Pete would be gone by the time I reached the battalion CP. The lieutenant looked as nervous as I; it seemed to me he was given the job in S-4 because he had become a bit jittery after he came back from the hospital. He was a Okie and they were trying to protect their own as best they could. Who could blame him for being a little edgy? Who wasn't? As we got closer to the front, the whistle of the shells going by overhead got louder and louder, so I started to drive with one foot out of the jeep, ready to make an instant dive if any of the whistles seemed to be coming in our direction. Thinking I was riding the clutch, the lieutenant told me not to ride the clutch so much. That ignorant Okie. I had driven a truck and owned a car five years before my entrance into the army. He probably hadn't even been in the front seat of any vehicle before he got into the army. I didn't miss a bump during that tortuous ride. That S.O.B. of a battalion commander, he would want to stage a raid with Tommy guns just when I got a nice soft job. Personally I think he was also testing the lieutenant to see if he had the guts to come up to the front and not just send the driver.

Finally we reached the crossroad where battalion headquarters was located. The enemy was known to drop a shell at this point every three or four minutes, and one better be out of the area as soon as an incoming shell exploded. As soon as we passed the crossroad, I turned onto the road where battalion was dug in. The lieutenant got out and said to wait there while he went down to battalion headquarters to find out where the Tommy guns were to be delivered. As I waited, I wondered how the hell I got into this situation! Here on top of this road where I had feared to walk in the past, I was sitting waiting to drive somewhere. As I was about to jump out of the jeep a soldier appeared and said he was a runner for K Company, and to follow him which was unusually hard as he walked very slow and half bent down. I expected him to start crawling. With one foot on the gas and the other out of the jeep, he led me across the road and walked or almost crept between two strands of white tape. This designated our own minefields. Luckily no machine guns opened up as I drove along or that would have been the end. He suddenly stopped and I saw a faint light; it was coming out of a dugout. I scrambled out of the jeep and into the dugout which turned out to be K Company's CP, The captain greeted me like a long-lost friend, and invited me to have a cup of coffee, which tasted unusually good. Lighting up a cigarette, I waited while the Tommy guns were unloaded. The captain was in unusually good spirits for someone whose company was going into a small skirmish in an hour or so.

After about fifteen minutes, it seemed to me it was about time to get out of there, but the captain wanted to talk. I couldn't blame him, but as long as it was quiet, with only a few flares lighting up the sky, it was a good time to get the hell out of there. So making the proper apologies, I got into the jeep and almost being afraid to start it up for fear the Germans would hear the motor and start machine-gunning the area with a few mortars thrown in. As I started to turn the jeep around in the narrow bounds between the two white pieces of tape, a bright light suddenly appeared in the sky. Flares were being shot up. It could be by either side; it was one way of noticing it any troops were trying to move forward or any unusual activities that could give a clue as to the portent of an attack. Not wanting to be outlined in the darkness, thus enabling an enemy observer to bring mortar or artillery fire down upon me, I froze where I was, ready to dive for the dugout if I heard any familiar whistles. After about five minutes as the last lingering light of the flares tell upon an almost cemetery-like silence, it became apparent to me that it was time to get going, and with as little noise as possible. The jeep moved forward, with my head stuck out the side as low as possible and for a moment anyone who could have seen me would have thought they were seeing a contortionist as my head almost touched my left leg which was half out of the jeep.

Slowly the jeep nosed forward until finally the open field came into contact with the road. Turning left and heading down the road, I knew that battalion headquarters was dug into the embankment on the other side and if the enemy fire got too hot, it would be nothing to abandon the jeep and find shelter along any part of the embankment. However I wasn't going to wait for the lieutenant up on the road and be exposed the way he left me to wait for the runner on the way to deliver the Tommy guns. Continuing down the road to the intersection where a turn to the right would start me back from where this journey had started and a second right would bring me alongside the embankment and that's the way the jeep went as I wasn't going to wait for the lieutenant on the open road. Just as the jeep came to a halt, machine gun fire raced across the open road ahead. Crouching down, my legs moved at a leisurely pace as the bullets flew past at a higher level. Artillery shells would have brought a different reaction. Moving along, a few of the men who were in the same company spotted me and asked what I was doing there. They thought I had a soft job in the rear. Does this look soft? That was my answer. Telling them the story of my second night in the rear, they all laughed. Knowing the perilous journey back to the easy life, there was doubt on my part that they envied my evening's work. Reaching the battalion CP, the lieutenant was inside enjoying a cup of coffee in the relative safety or the dugout. He was supposed to have gone along with me. To hell with the yellow son of a bitch. My mind was only on getting back to our palace in the rear. It was almost an uneventful trip back, devoid of flares. The enemy artillery gunners must have gone for a smoke, and the German planes that earlier had been dropping personnel bombs must have taken the rest of the night off.

The next day, having missed breakfast because we slept until about noon (what a life) I was on my way to eat lunch, when who should I bump into but Neil Shea. He was in the 1st battalion, but the motor pools were adjacent to each other. His hole wasn't more than 30 yards away. It was a happy reunion. When I told him I was taking the job of the jeep driver for the battalion S-4 for a week or so, he asked me to sleep in his dugout. Asking the lieutenant if it was all right, he nodded his approval. Going over to Neil's dugout, it wasn't what I would call shell-proof. Immediately, I started filling sandbags to shore up the entrance and the sides. That would take up this slack of exploding shells and would protect against almost any explosion except a direct hit. The first night together we went over letters from home and any local events that had occurred since we had last seen each other. After dinner, as a delicacy I opened a can of sardines that I had acquired from a British soldier in exchange for a couple of K rations. It was almost an uneventful night, except for a number of shells that exploded nearby. This was in response to the shelling done by the tanks of the 1st Armored Division, which was less than 50 yards from our position. The next morning we didn't awaken until about 10 A.M. and might have been still sleeping if the sounds of shovels hadn't awakened us. Getting out of our dugout, and not 10 yards away, about twenty soldiers were digging and lugging dirt out of what had been a dugout. Going over to find out what had happened, one soldier told us that the two sergeants that had inhabited the dugout had been killed during the night. The dugout had received a direct hit, but the sergeants hadn't been killed by shrapnel, but by suffocation. I had noticed an over-abundance of sandbags on top of their dugout the previous day. The sandbags had fallen in on them and they suffocated. It was easier to die in Anzio than to stay alive. Neil wanted to dig a new hole, closer to where the sergeants had dug theirs. There was the evidence one could get killed in the rear almost as easy as one could get killed at the front.

The next two nights passed without incident. There was the usual artillery barrage from the tanks of the 1st Armored Division during the day and the return German fire at night with the ammunition dumps set ablaze every evening giving us a front-seat view of a fireworks display to fill in our entertainment schedule. Laying in a dugout in the rear had its compensations, but one had to pay a price at times. So it was with some drivers attached to the motor pool; they would take turns driving up to the front at different nights to haul up ammunition if their job demanded it. So it was one night as Neil and I were talking about the good old days back home in our dugout, when out of the dark came a call for Shea—a most unwelcome call if one's name happened to be Shea. Neil turned away from the opening in the dugout, as if that could stop the sound of the sergeant's voice from entering our sanctuary. Driving up to the front was as bad as playing Russian roulette. I had undergone that danger the second night that I was in the rear. Going up to the front was a scary experience but I was going back to where I usually hung out. However, for anyone going to a place where all kinds of stories of the most horrendous kind filled the air in the rear; psychologically, one was defeated before one started the journey. Even if a truce was announced, the person going to the front would be under such a strain that such a person would do anything not to have to make the trip. It took an unusual amount of courage to answer the call to drive to the front.

"Neil," I said, "your sergeant is calling. You better answer."

He replied, "The hell with him. It's someone else's turn." But the name Shea kept ringing out as if it was on a record machine.

"Neil, you better answer the bastard," I said, though it was none of my business. Probably the sergeant had tried to get another driver and couldn't find whose turn it was and turned to his patsy who he knew would finally answer and that was the exact situation that had happened. One of the other drivers whose turn it was didn't answer, so Neil was forced to take his place. Crawling out of the hole with nothing but profanity emitting from his mouth as he denounced both his sergeant and the driver who didn't show up for his turn, Neil puffed furiously on a cigarette, and said good-bye in the dark night. I felt sorry that he had to go. It's funny, but one can fall asleep under the most trying circumstances after having spent a considerable time at the front, and that's what I did, not knowing if Neil would ever come back.

I must have slept a couple of hours when I was awakened by the most vile profanity. Neil was crawling back into the dugout, and at the same time was denouncing the sergeant who had called him, not counting the Nazi bastards. Lighting up a cigarette, we continued our conversation as if he had never been away.

The next morning after going to where our mess sergeant had established his kitchen, I was surprised to see one of the other members of my platoon having coffee there. "What the hell are you doing here?" I asked.

"I came back to relieve you," he brusquely replied.

"This is a temporary job that the 1st sergeant assigned me to. What's that got to do with the platoon?"

He answered, "Well the lieutenant said it was like a rest camp and all the other guys said it wasn't fair for you to be back here all the time, so the lieutenant thought every one should take a turn. You're supposed to go back up with the mess sergeant tonight." He had come back with him the previous night.

I didn't really give a shit because I knew the supply lieutenant's driver would be coming back from Naples any day, but those jealous bastards in my platoon; two of the sergeants had been latrine flunkies back in the States when I was practically platoon sergeant and none of them could set off a dynamite explosion. To further have complications, we had to have a Jewish platoon lieutenant who had come up to us in Anzio when the Irish lieutenant was given a break and sent off the beachhead. Give me the Irish lieutenant. The Jewish lieutenant by name of Ostroff figured he had to bend backwards not to offend the other members of the platoon because I was also Jewish. Who needed him? He had been full of pep and vinegar when he came up, but he hadn't had the shit scared out of him for the last eight months, so he wasn't as shell-shocked as the rest of us. Therefore, to show his impartiality he ordered me to rejoin the platoon.

That night I went up with the mess sergeant in his jeep. As soon as I got off in the rear battalion CP, Kovaly, whose squad I was supposed to be in, ordered me to go up to the forward battalion CP. He said I had enough rest. Ostroff was standing right there. At least I should have stayed there overnight, but who gave a shit? After telling them what I thought about them, I got back in the jeep with John, the mess sergeant, and we took off for the forward battalion CP. I had driven up there myself earlier in the week, so it didn't bother me to go up, but it was the way it was done.

Arriving at the forward battalion headquarters I felt almost at home. There are times when one feels he has arrived at a place where one belongs. I reported to no one, except a dugout that was dug into the side of an embankment that made up a part of the road that traversed that part of our front. That first night I slept alone, not that it bothered me, but the job that we were to perform was to lay barbed wire, stand guard, lay explosives, or be thrown into the line like ordinary riflemen. However since the action was at a lull, it wasn't too hard to take. The next night I had a partner. Fiakovich was sent up to keep me company, but during the day I got acquainted with different members of my company. There were men from the antitank platoon, the communication platoon, and the intelligence section. Almost everyone in the company seemed glad to see me. I did get information from Smitty, who was in communications. I had known him from Camp Pickett. Everyone seemed to be under an unusual strain. I soon found out it was the new or practically new battalion commander, Colonel Webber. He was on everyone's back, whether it was demanding that everyone shave everyday, which was ludicrous, or trying to straighten out our lines. When he had asked for the Tommy guns which I had brought up earlier in the week, and that little action had caused five men to be killed and I didn't know how many wounded, Colonel Webber had become a problem. To be around the area where Colonel Webber was holed up could be real dangerous. No one knew when he would demand a patrol go out and see what the enemy was doing and anyone could be chosen for this sought-after type off work.

One night when our sector was under heavy artillery fire, I saw Lieutenant Ostroff and Sergeant Blake come out of the CP. Asking where they were going, I was told they were going to go down the road to start a fire and maybe the Germans would see the fire and throw their artillery fire in that direction and away from our battalion lines. They did start the fire and it could be seen for quite a distance, but the Germans weren't fooled; they kept directing their artillery fire on our lines. They should have known that the enemy already having hit something and set it on fire wouldn't waste shell fire on something already burning. Brains were a luxury with most officers.

A few days later about a half dozen soldiers were brought up to our positions. They were guarded by regimental MPs. The MPs handed them over to us and said they were sent up to the lines because they had run away from their companies while under fire and their punishment was to be sent up to the front and made to do whatever dangerous jobs had to be done, such as laying barbed wire, probably setting down a few mines, or whatever other job could be found for them. Once they were turned over to us, they asked where they were to stay. We told them they had to dig their own dugouts as there wasn't anything available for guests. Starting immediately to dig in, these soldiers wasted no time as they picked a most undesirable spot, as far as I was concerned. Their spot had been a place situated under the culvert. They dug into the concrete with abandon; they would have made good engineers. Every time a shell would come over, their digging got more furious. These soldiers pulled stone after stone out of that section of the culvert where they had been digging out of when to my amazement they finished, and the six of them scurried into their new home.

Now these men weren't some ordinary deserters, such as those men who came up to the line and then ran away after a few days; they all sported ribbons which denoted that they had the Purple Heart, Bronze or Silver Star. They had been around a while and the pressure had gotten to be too much for them. They all came out of rifle companies; it was too bad. Thousands of men were back in the

Naples area doing absolutely nothing and could have been sent up to the lines at Anzio to fill in, and these men could have been sent back to perform their duties, such as they were; such is the injustice of war. The general was going to teach men like this a lesson; they were too far gone psychologically to be of value to anyone in a combat area. Coming out of their dugout, all of them kept yelling, "Give me a court-martial and I'll take Alcatraz gladly." We all smiled; they weren't so stupid. Alcatraz sounded good to me. After handing out a few packages of cigarettes to these men, our conversation got friendly. They all had been in Sicily and with the division through Italy and into Anzio, but how long can one last under these conditions was their stark question. This subject had gone through my mind many times.

The following night we started out to lay barbed wire and these men were to do the work while we were to stand guard over them. Slowly, we moved out of our position and moved forward across the road and past the rifle companies. The prisoners carried the wire, although they were quiet; their stumbling around seemed to set off more noise than one likes to hear so close to the enemy lines. A few enemy flares lit up the sky and we all hit the ground, lying as motionless as the ground underneath us. The minute the light of the flares faded we were up and moving forward reaching the position where the barbed wire was to be laid. The prisoners were told to come forward and start their work. Not one of them had laid barbed wire or even knew what to do. After a moment or two of exasperation, I grabbed a couple of stakes from one of them, handed over my rifle to him, and proceeded to put the stakes into the ground. The other men did the same after handing over their rifles, grabbing the barbed wire and we all proceeded to lay it down while the prisoners, holding our rifles, looked on. What a reversal of positions, but who the hell was going to wait around an area where it was almost as dangerous as swimming with sharks, while these men took lessons in how to lay barbed wire? It was a most comical situation; that is, for onlookers from a safe distance. Luck was with us. The enemy had seemed to run out of flares and our job was completed in record time. Gingerly, we started back, retracing our steps, as there were minefields in the area. Finally, our dugouts loomed out to us—what a welcome sight! Even though the front had been unusually quiet that night, after getting my rifle back from the prisoner I had given it to, a smile came over my face. What if he had taken off again? How could I explain that I had let him hold my rifle? They all scurried into their dugout and the rest of us just went to our dugouts and lit up well-deserved cigarettes. The prisoners continued to talk about "Silent Maries" mortar shells. They were different because one didn't even hear the whistles. Those shells just plopped down. The prisoners had a phobia about mortars. Who could blame them—especially if one had been caught in an open field which was being boxed in with mortar fire?

The next morning, the prisoners came out from their sanctuary under the culvert. Bright and eager, they seemed to have lost some of their fear, but they started to be back in their semi-comical form asking for a court-martial and to be sent to Alcatraz upon being found guilty. They made all of us laugh.

The week passed unusually fast, and with the end of the week came the end of the presence of the prisoners. They had gotten their wish; they were going to be court-martialed, but I doubt their punishment was a major calamity. Most men were left with minor punishments and then assigned to a rear echelon unit and there whiled away the war. However, there were exceptions to that rule. No sooner had the prisoners been taken away when a replacement was sent up and given a hole right next to mine. I don't know who the hell he replaced, but he started to cry the moment he was shown the dugout where he was to stay. That first night his crying was incessant, and every time enemy shell fire exploded close to us, his wailing became almost unbearable. Certainly he was a danger to our side; the enemy probably could hear his wailing and it made it that much easier for them to pinpoint our positions with artillery fire. When daylight came, this soldier never came out of his hole. That night he was sent back with the mess sergeant, probably even off the beachhead and back to Naples, where he could boast about being up at the front and even be awarded a few medals. Later, he probably got a pension as a psycho, while the men who had been. sent up as prisoners after running away from the lines would most likely have the court-martial on their record. If I only had gotten that S.O.B.'s name I surely would let everyone know. He probably would be the one who would march in all the parades. It wouldn't be anything new. Parades and most veterans' organizations had as their most active members those who had experienced very little combat.

It was getting warmer and there was more light during the day; that is, fewer hours of darkness, so we would stand against the embankment and gaze at the enemy lines or the sky. So one day looking up at the upper atmosphere, I was watching one of our piper cubs. Those were the small planes that directed artillery fire upon the enemy from the air; they did an unusually good job of pinpointing enemy artillery pieces. The men in those planes showed an unusual amount of courage. Everyday they were flying over enemy lines seeking out the enemy's positions and directing our artillery fire down on the Nazi S.O.B.s. They were always under fire; I always admired those men, but really never got a chance to meet them. This day that I was watching this plane fly lazily over the enemy lines, an unusual occurrence happened. While watching this particular plane maneuver over the enemy, it disintegrated into the air right before my eyes. The parts of the plane flew in all directions. For a moment I wondered what had happened. Had an enemy 88-mm shell hit it? But they flew so low; they were out of reach of the enemy's shell fire. It had to be one of our artillery shells, and as I later found out, it was one of our shells that tore into the piper cub. It was a freak accident, one in a million; and to my surprise it was written up later in a piece in the *Stars & Stripes* by Ernie Pyle.

The Germans kept up their heavy artillery fire for a few days and tried to break through our lines in a local area which was where I happened to be residing. They were unsuccessful, but as the week wore on their artillery was particularly active. So one night when I had fallen asleep someone started to shake me; it was Fiakovich.

"What the hell do you want?" I said as I woke from a most sound sleep.

"Do you hear that tank on the road above us?" he asked.

"So what?" I answered.

"Listen to him throw those 88 shells down on us," he whispered.

Sure enough, shells were falling on our side of the embankment and exploding with a tremendous sound. "What the hell did you wake me up for?" I asked.

"I was scared listening to them shells exploding and the tank above scared the shit out of me, and if I was going to be scared, I didn't want to be alone so you might as well be scared with me."

"You son of a bitch," I said. "Here I was sleeping soundly and didn't even hear the exploding shells and now you get me moving up and down as each shell explodes closer to our hole. You bastard." I called him every other profanity I could think of. I was mad. Now we both sweated out this artillery barrage in our cramped dugout. I told him I would kick the shit out of him for waking me up, but he was lucky, the shells were exploding right outside our front door. After a most terrifying two hours or so of this attack, things quieted down. Falling asleep for a few minutes and then awaking as dawn broke, I reached for my canteen, which I always kept right outside the hole at night because the cold night kept the water cold and the cold water always felt good going down my esophagus after all the smoking that my tonsils tasted the past twelve hours or so. As I reached out and pulled my canteen into the dugout, it felt unusually light even though it had been filled the previous evening when the mess sergeant had come up with our rations and water. Taking off the cover in the half light of my hole and lifting the canteen to my lips, no water came out.

Fiakovich yelled, "It's full of holes!" Sure enough as I lifted it into the light, the canteen looked more like a sieve than a canteen. It was full of holes; the shrapnel had rained outside our hole for half the night and my canteen had become a casualty. It deserved the Purple Heart. I had another reason to curse the Germans that morning.

Fiakovich started to tell the story of my ill-fated canteen to one of the communications soldiers when he was interrupted by the same soldier with a story of his own, One fellow from I Company had shot himself in the foot during the night. His fellow companion in their dugout went for their platoon leader instead of a medic. The lieutenant took the soldier's shoe off so he could see how bad he was hit. When the shoe came off, there was no wound, even though the tip of the shoe had a bullet hole in it. As luck would have it, it was an army shoe and they were usually a half-size too big. The bullet had gone through the shoe but not the toes. "Better luck next time," the lieutenant remarked as he walked away smiling. *C'est le guerre*. That's the way it was; it took plenty of nerve to shoot oneself, and then finding out one had missed his target. The result must have been devastating. This wasn't the first time someone I knew had attempted to shoot himself. My friend from New Bedford, who I had been in training camp with back in the States and had waited back in a repo-depot in Sicily to join our outfit also shot himself in the leg, but was more successful then the I Company soldier. A fellow I knew from his company told me he got a letter from his sister telling him how this soldier was back home telling everyone how he had been shot by the enemy. How the hell did he get home so fast? The bullets, bombs, and artillery shells could drive a person to do desperate things! It never crossed my mind to get involved in such an escapade. I would rather take my chances with the enemy shooting me than shooting myself. Anyway I didn't have the courage to pull the trigger on myself.

It was May; the days were getting warmer and the heavy action all seemed to be on the Casino front, so the news from the *Star & Stripes* was filled with the latest offensive action from that front. Our battlefield seemed to be quiet compared to what it had been, but it was only the quiet before the storm. Outside of a few patrols sent out to keep an eye on the enemy and a few artillery shells passing overhead, these early days of May became almost bearable. Of course, our flamboyant Colonel Webber had to have a look at the enemy lines, so taking a couple of soldiers with him he went out to one of our OPs (observation posts). The story goes that he stuck his hand up to have a look at the enemy through his binoculars and was shot through his head by a sniper. There was a story going around that he had been shot by one of his own men. That seemed almost as plausible as the sniper story, as there was no love lost between the men of the battalion and Webber.

The next morning after the colonel's demise most everyone was smiling around the forward battalion CP; it seemed like a load had been lifted off everyone's shoulders.

Things started to happen right after that. An order came down to be ready to move to another sector as the British were going to take over our lines.

The next morning about an hour before dawn, someone came by our dugout and told us to be ready to move in about ten minutes. The army is nuts; ten minutes to move from a place that I had occupied for almost a month. All was quiet as I looked out into the darkness of the early morning, and then as I got out of my dugout, I wanted to jump back in. About 30 yards from our position where the roads intersected were vehicles with their dark lights on. We could see men smoking. Were these men nuts? For the last month we had practically walked around on our tiptoes and the only time one smoked was in his dugout. The enemy could see and hear any noise or light for miles, and that was a sure way to get the Germans to throw in an artillery barrage. These British troops were nuts; they were so complacent, even an earthquake wouldn't arouse them to any emotion.

Grabbing my carbine and what few personal belongings I had, I moved quickly and quietly past the British trucks lined up on the road. Walking for about an hour, our line finally reached a point on the beachhead that was only about a mile or so from the water. Daybreak was upon us as we reached our designated bivouac. As most of the men sat down and relaxed, it was quite noticeable that each man wasn't too far from a dugout. Those dugouts had sprouted up all over the beachhead; experience taught us that a hole in the ground that was close by was one way of staying alive a little longer.

The mess sergeant had hot coffee waiting. What a way to live.

Everyone seemed exhausted but the future looked bright; troops from the Casino front had broken through to connect with our men at Anzio and it seemed as though the breakout was imminent. In fact, our division had been squeezed out of the line by the British; therfore, we would be resting for a few days until the breakout was to start.

Fresh troops came on to Anzio from the south transported by ships; among them was the 442 Regiment made up of Japanese-Americans. It was one of the best fighting regiments in the army, and we automatically knew it would be used for a spearhead. In our company was a soldier named Toy; by a quirk he had been assigned to our battalion. I think he was the only American of Japanese descent who wasn't assigned to the 442 Regiment. He was a wonderful, gentle, and kind fellow and he later became mess sergeant of our company. His brother, who was a lieutenant in the 442 Regiment, came over to visit Toy, so that is how I met him. He probably was no more than 21, a nice young fellow; and it was funny that after Toy introduced his brother, conversation went on as if we had known each other for years. That is the way people who have been in combat get to be. Here was a nice young American boy of Japanese descent from Hawaii, who if he was back in the States would be refused admission to the VFW or American Legion and yet he was ready to die for his country, which he did on the breakout from the Anzio beach. Toy was informed of the death of his brother by some of his friends when we reached Rome.

After lying around for a few days basking in the late-May Italian sun, the regiment was alerted and we started to move forward to take up positions closer to the front. The battalion moved past our former static positions where we had been dug in for over four months, past the railroad and into whose embankments the Germans had their dugouts.

Huge railroad trestles covered their dugouts. No wonder even bombs didn't knock them out of commission, but a horrendous smell emanated from these homes away from homes. Bodies of uncounted Germans were still in these holes; the bombardment on the breakout had been tremendous, and the Nazis hadn't had a chance to salvage their dead.

Our platoon set up guard duty around the rear battalion C P, while the rest of the battalion moved forward. Our position was on a hill that overlooked a valley, and one could see for a few miles to our right and beyond. As I settled down by a former German dugout, I lit up a cigarette and looked down into the valley, and much to my surprise, a British artillery unit that consisted of 25 pounders, an artillery weapon similar to our 155-mm guns, started unloading their trucks of ammunition and detaching the guns that had been hauled by their trucks. In no time, they had set up their guns and unloaded their ammunition. It wasn't any more than fifteen minutes and the guns were firing. Those British soldiers were amazing; it was like watching a war movie. Then tragedy struck. As I watched from a distance of about a half mile away on a ledge overlooking the valley, it was like sitting on the 50-yard line at a football game. A puff of smoke emitted from the ammunition dump the British had set up a few yards from their guns. Then an explosion and the ammunition blew up; the artillery guns were lifted high into the air as if they were a few feathers being blown around by a light breeze. Those poor British soldiers; they must have been blown to bits. Their artillery guns were blown into the air as if they were toys. It must have been a lucky hit from a German mortar or Howitzer. We could see them; the Germans must have been able to get a good glimpse of their ammunition dump. They were too close to the front for an artillery battery.

While we waited, some of the fellows started a poker game in a dugout, which was a natural cave. They called me in to play and so I did. As the game progressed, some of the players went broke and left the game. Berrey was one of them. About ten minutes later he came back to the game with some money. I asked if somebody had loaned him the money. No one had. One of the fellows said there was a dead German soldier down the path with his pockets turned inside out, as if someone had been searching the body. Then I questioned Berrey. Again, he refused to answer. Taking that as a yes, I got up and refused to play, not because the money came from a dead German, but I remembered what had happened to the soldier who had laughed when he heard Subverri was missing in action. Maybe I had become a little superstitious, but I wasn't playing poker with a dead man's money; that's when I got up and walked outside. A few minutes later a messenger came up from the battalion CP. They wanted someone to go down there to be available to carry messages to the front. Kosally picked me immediately because I had left the game. It was a sort of a punishment, but it turned out to be a blessing.

I moved slowly down the path keeping in mind that the Germans could catch a glimpse of me as I worked my way toward the battalion CP, just as they had spotted the British artillery battery. But finally I reached the CP; the Captain was standing outside.

"You're the messenger, I presume."

"That's me," I answered, with as little respect as possible. He was the bastard who had busted me to private back in the States. Telling me to relax and hang around the front of the CP, he went inside. As I relaxed smoking a cigarette, my whole platoon came marching by with Kosally and Hook in the front. Hook asked me if I wanted to change places with him; they had been ordered to fill in for a rifle company at the front. There was a shortage of men; I had just missed becoming a rifleman because of a dead German soldier's money. I smiled as they went by swearing; for once I had been lucky.

Lying by the CP entrance all the noise or battle was just up the hill. Then on the scene appeared one of the men from the platoon; he had been made a sergeant on Anzio. He deserved that promotion as much as the dead German soldier laying down the road deserved to be alive. He was yelling and screaming while he held his ears as if he had been shell-shocked. "Where's the Medics?" he yelled.

"Down the path." I told him to take it easy and sit down, hoping this would calm him. This was the last time I saw him. He probably made his way back home; I didn't believe him, maybe the medics did.

As I sat there, another soldier appeared. He seemed to be shaking. I knew him because he had been with the company before I had joined. He was from Oklahoma, and was with the antitank platoon. He had been in the hospital in Africa and I don't know how long he had been gone from the company, but he was bitching how he had to come back while some soldiers who were Jewish were still there. I guess he didn't know I was Jewish.

"You yellow bastard," I said. "Look how long you were gone and you're still bitching. You should be up at the front, not down here."

With this outburst from me, he slithered away to the other side of the battalion CP. He probably wondered why I opened up on him the way I did. Lying down to wait for further orders, a yell came out of the CP. We had been ordered to move up and join the rest of the company. Moving forward rapidly, we came up on the front line with some of the troops lying in open foxholes looking exhausted. The enemy had pulled back; orders were to continue to move forward, and we did. The battalion was on the move and as we walked down a narrow road, there in front of us were a line of our tanks with smoke emanating from every one of them. As I passed by, I could see that each tank had been knocked out by enemy fire and had been set on fire. They had been caught in a narrow pass; the first tank had been knocked out and blocked the road. This made the other tanks easy targets; that was certainly poor leadership on the part of the one in charge of these tanks.

Moving forward slowly, everyone seemed to feel as if they had been liberated from a prison. After all when one has been under constant fire from artillery and planes and usually jumps into a dugout, stationary positions become a habit. But now we were moving forward in spite of a whistle or two from artillery fire, and the whish of a bullet going past; it became a most enjoyable walk. Nightfall was almost upon us and so the company started to look for a place to dig in for the night. Picking a place on the side of an incline, I started to dig in. Digging foxholes had become an automatic habit. Besides it was good for one's health; better to be safe than sorry when those artillery shells began splattering around and throwing off their life-ending shrapnel. Tired to the point of exhaustion, I soon fell asleep. It seemed like only minutes, but hours had passed. I was awakened by the sound of trucks and tanks going by. Trucks, were going by at a fast pace. The enemy had been in front of us only a few hours earlier, but it was breaking down and trucks were rolling along the road below my foxhole.

There were a few shouted orders emanating in the area; men were moving down from the hill and started moving in two columns along the road as a warm June sun helped drive the chill of the preceding night from the bones of the men as they started walking along the road.

There were smiles on almost every face of the GIs who formed the column marching toward Rome.

As we moved along, there were signs posted along the road. Appian Way was printed on one of these road signs. Unbelievable—I was walking on the Appian Way. That was a road built by the Romans more than two thousand years ago. The stone or bricks that made up the road were still intact. My mind went back to my high school days and the Latin courses that I had taken under Mr. Shea and Mr. Hertell. Could this be the Appian Way of Caesar and the Romans that they had taught me about? I yelled out at a few of the fellows; we're on the Appian Way. Do you know what that means? I might as well have been trying to explain one of Verdi's operas, but at least I knew I was treading on ground where the Roman armies had marched, more than two thousand years earlier.

Houses soon appeared on two sides of the road. Signs for Rome appeared. As the sun set higher, I could tell we were walking in a northwesterly direction and our regiment was circling Rome to the west. Suddenly another historical sight appeared. We had come upon a small body of water. There was part of a bridge that crossed over this small stream. Whoever had tried to blow up this edifice had done a poor job. On a signpost bore the name Tiber River. My God, Caesar had crossed the Tiber, but not Hannibal; and here I was about to go over this famous river. The other men thought I had become shell-shocked or plain nuts because of the exuberance I had shown when we came upon the Appian Way, and now the Tiber. In fact, I don't think they had ever heard of these two sites. As I walked across this partly demolished bridge, my mind started to wander. All of a sudden I was a soldier in a Roman legion going to fight the Carthaginians; but wait, Hannibal had been one of my heroes. He had crossed the Alps with elephants, more than over 2,200 years earlier. This daydreaming better stop or some sniper will get a clear shot at me, I thought. Worse yet, one misstep and down into the Tiber I could go. Getting to the other side, our battalion moved along for a few more miles and moved up to some hilly ground. We waited at this point for the battalion commander to get there. He was the 4th battalion commander we had since we arrived at Anzio. Two had been killed, one badly wounded, and this latest one had taken over just before we entered Rome.

Upon his arrival in his jeep we walked over to see what orders he was going to give. Instead he got out and said. "Let's go looking for a location to set up the battalion CP. As we walked, a few bullets whizzed by and fell harmlessly in the surrounding grass. The snipers must have been at least a mile away as their bullets had lost their power, or so it seemed. After all, who was afraid of being sniped at with bullets when one had been sniped at with artillery shells for the past four months?

So in this hilly area overlooking Rome, the battalion settled down for the night. As I lay down in the grass, night had fallen and a full moon seemed to fill the sky. "Fiakovich," I said, "that's an invasion moon; the second front can't be far away. Maybe tomorrow morning." So ended June 5, the day Rome fell.

"Syd, Syd," someone yelled while pulling at my shoulders trying to wake me.

With one eye opened, I stared out at a bright sun. "What the hell is the matter with you guys?" Before I could start using profanity, I heard the words "Invasion! Invasion! France has been invaded from England!" That was good news; here was one invasion in Europe that I missed. It felt good to think that someone else was on a beach lighting up a cigarette and then sitting up to a bright sun with the surrounding air partly filled with the chirping of birds instead of the whistle of incoming artillery shells.

For a change this morning, there were no whistles of artillery shells. The clattering of machine guns were missing and my ears were getting back to normal. What was more unusual I had slept on open ground all night and not dug into the ground like a scared animal.

Sitting up now and conversing with some of the fellows about the invasion of Normandy was all the excitement that was generated that morning. Then the breakfast call went out. Slowly the men moved toward the area where the kitchen was set up, and walked-timidly as if they were expecting a barrage to start at any moment. Four months of continuous artillery barrages can't be erased by the passing of one day. As the men passed through the mess line there seemed to be a party mood emerging. No one talked about the past horrendous months at Anzio, but the conversation was pointed to how long we would be able to relax at this position. Everyone was satisfied to be left alone and just left to relax and get his senses back. As I passed other men of the company looking for a place to eat we nodded at each other, as if to say "Glad you've made it and are still alive." Much can be said with a nod. We didn't talk about the men no longer with us.

CHAPTER TWELVE

Rome

Two days had passed; the regiment was still in place and no one cared whether any orders came through again to move on. Then an announcement came from the 1st sergeant that the regimental colonel was to say a few words to the whole regiment in a valley in the Roman hills the next day.

Walking to the meeting, the troops seemed to be on their way to a political meeting in their hometown, instead of being under military order to meet that day. When the men had all settled into sitting or standing positions, the colonel started speaking. "Every man in this regiment is going to see Rome; this is an opportunity not to be missed, and if anyone doesn't get into Rome for any reason, come see me and I'll take you in personally." I was impressed by that speech. Rome was something I didn't intend to miss.

The next day I went over to see if Neil Shea had survived the break through. After arriving at his battalion, it didn't take me long to find him. Off we went, heading for Rome. Army trucks were almost as plentiful as the grass in the fields; it wasn't long before I could smoke a second cigarette. The driver was letting us off near St. Peter's Square. It didn't take long to find St. Peter's Cathedral. Neil and I went in, and without guides managed to take a complete three-hour tour of our own; it was an exhilarating experience, and even more profound for Neil Shea.

After our tour of St. Peter's, like other tourists we started out to see the sights of Rome. We were without cash, but carried something more exchangeable—tobacco products. With a few packages of Camels at a store that dealt in liquor and other sundry products, I was able to obtain a fair-sized bottle of cherry brandy and anisette. Neil had brought along some Bull Durham; one made cigarettes out of that tobacco. I couldn't stop laughing when he produced two bags of Bull Durham to barter for alcoholic beverages. I hadn't seen Bull Durham for years. Asking him what he was doing with that kind of tobacco, he answered perfectly innocently that was all that he had been able to obtain from his mess sergeant. What was most outstanding were the number of tourist attractions we got to see in one day, from Mussolini's balcony to the Coliseum, to the tomb of the Unknown Soldier, to the Roman ruins where we sat on the wall and gazed down on what had been Rome 2,000 years earlier while we slowly sipped the alcoholic beverages that we had obtained earlier in the day. We didn't go unnoticed by the local citizenry as they attempted to converse with us. How we got back to our respective companies that evening is still a mystery.

The next morning while eating breakfast I related my experience of the previous day in Rome. All of a sudden there was an outpouring of invitations to accompany some of the men to Rome that morning. Al Hook, Dunns, and I took off right after breakfast but fortified with a few extra packs of cigarettes and K rations thrown in, just in case our tobacco products weren't enough to buy what we might want. So after shaving a second day in a row, off to the eternal city and new adventures.

This time, with a little experience under my belt, we tried to catch a horse-drawn carriage to see the sights of Rome. As a carriage drove by, I pulled out two K rations and a couple of packs of cigarettes, waving them wildly at the cab driver. Sure enough, he stopped abruptly, as if an iron gate had come down in from of his horse. Running over before he changed his mind, we all jumped into the cab, telling him we would give him two K rations now and two when were through for the day, plus the same number of packs of cigarettes. He immediately took off with us as passengers. This time I saw the same sights that I had seen the previous day, but from the advantage of a sitting position in a horse-drawn cab and the liquor we acquired that day tasted better from a sitting position. We did get to see one sight that I had missed the previous day—the Spanish Steps. This view of the Spanish Steps was by an around-about way as the cab driver had brought us up to a hotel on a hill that overlooked them. We had met some British soldiers and they invited us into the hotel. We told the driver to wait, holding the remaining K rations and cigarettes as a guarantee he would wait for us. As we entered the hotel, there was music and singing in the lobby and we joined in by offering our cherry brandy to the English soldiers. Coming out of the hotel, the carriage was right where we left it, with the driver sleeping in the back. Al Hook was yelling at me for giving most of our liquor to the British, but who cared? Everyone was still celebrating the capture of Rome, three days after the event.

There was only one instance that had marred our day in Rome. While riding around Rome in the horse-drawn cab, three soldiers had tried to take over the vehicle, but with stubborn resistance we held on to our prize while the driver seemed to enjoy the encounter with American soldiers pitted against American soldiers.

How we got back to our camp, I'll never know but as I got almost to the top of the incline where I had laid out my equipment, I slipped and fell backwards, rolling rather than falling down this incline and into Kovaly's tent I went, my body knocking the tent and Kovaly all over. Kovaly didn't know what hit him; neither did I. Kovaly pulled himself out of his fallen tent, screaming nothing but profanity, army style. Who could blame him? He had been awakened from a sound sleep by a fully inebriated soldier. So with one hard jab on my shoulder, he pushed me down the rest of what remained of the incline, where I must have lain for a half hour before getting up and trying to walk up this small hill. This time I steadied myself when the top was reached, and with all the strength left in my arms, hurled my body over the top onto the plateau where my equipment lay and with final desperation thrust myself into what seemed like my blanket and immediately fell asleep under a chilly Rome sky.

I got up the next day for a late breakfast and early lunch as lunch was just being served. Conversation was limited to how the invasion of Normandy was going and how far the troops who had taken over from us had chased the Nazis up the Italian peninsula. The food was good; our mess sergeant was a good cook and a baker by trade. French bread and cupcakes were part of the menu.

Just as we finished eating, mail call was announced for the first time in over two weeks. Every one retired to their private boudoirs to read their mail. After going through my mail, my eyes closed and it was just at supper one of the fellows woke me to say it was time to eat again. What a life—nothing to do but relax and eat and listen to the radio which told of the fighting in France. What a pleasure to listen to how other soldiers were doing in combat.

The next day at breakfast, the first sergeant announced that anyone who wanted tickets to the show, "This Is the Army," by Irving Berlin should come to the battalion CP and pick them up. The play was at the Roman Opera House and combat troops had preference for the available seats.

After dinner, a few of us went over to the CP to pick up tickets for the show that evening. I went into Rome once more, but this tine to be seated and entertained, by Mr. Berlin. Arriving at the opera house, there were soldiers from noncombat outfits milling all around the building making really high bids for anyone willing to sell their tickets. Who needed anything that they had to offer? We had more than enough cigarettes to trade on our own. Our mess sergeant, while on Anzio had drawn rations for a full company of almost two hundred men, while the company most of the time was a little more than half strength, so rations were no problem. And if one wanted a few extra packs, he gladly handed them over to the men. He was perfectly honest and though he could have gone into Rome and garnered a small fortune by trading the rations, that never happened. This was the way it was in a combat outfit.

Walking into the opera house, ushers came up to where we were standing and with the utmost respect took our ticket stubs and we were seated in comfortable orchestra seats.

Irving Berlin's show was a fast-paced musical and well worth seeing, with Mr. Berlin himself doing a few numbers, and his rendition of "How I Hate to Get Up in the Morning" was really a show stopper.

After almost two weeks of doing nothing, word came down to our company that the division was going to move out, not into combat but further south and away from the combat area. This certainly was good news. Two days later, everyone was boarding trucks and we did move slowly south to, of all places, Anzio. Two weeks weren't enough to erase the nightmare of four months that I had spent on that battlefield. We were bivouacked in an open field with our blankets and the open sky.

The first evening at our new location, I looked with skepticism at the Alban hills. Those same hills had looked down upon me for four months and had hidden the Germans and their artillery shells which had rained down upon us without interruption during that period. From natural instinct I picked out the lowest piece of earth on the field, just in case there might be an artillery barrage from the enemy.

Once or twice I had awakened, and nervously looked around, half expecting artillery shells to be whistling by, but all was quiet. Most of the men were sleeping or so it seemed; surely they must be as nervous as I. Just then Sergeant Murphy got up and walked by. He had joined us after Anzio and was assigned to the antitank platoon. I remembered how he had joined the outfit only a few days ago. Filosi, who was the antitank platoon sergeant was taking him around and introducing him to different soldiers in the company. I was playing poker with Sergeant Frisby and some other men when I heard Murphy ask Filosi if there were any Jews in the company. I kind of moved but held my composure and then my mind went to the thought of the propaganda being passed around in the States about no Jews on the front. Filosi really answered for me as I could hear him tell Murphy that the man he was replacing, Penn was a Jew. He then introduced him to Fishman, Hendel, and me, and about six other Jews. He was startled as he walked away and I could hear him say "You can't believe everything you hear." It wasn't his fault that the propaganda was spread, but he found out the truth in good fashion. All the anti-Semites weren't in Germany. There were plenty in the States.

CHAPTER THIRTEEN

France

That morning we moved out to the sea and got on LSTs and they took us back to the Salerno area. It seems we were going back the way we had come. We disembarked from the ships and set up tents in an open field. Outside of a few military necessities, the men were practically free to wander in whatever direction they wished. There were many trips organized by the battalion to take the men to many historic places—Pompeii, Herculaneum, and even to Mount Vesuvius.

I personally picked out a town called Tora Del Greco, where cameos were made and a dollar could buy the best around. I used to go to a restaurant that overlooked the Bay of Naples. It was a beautiful spot and for a dollar had steak and fried potatoes and one more dollar bought a bottle of cherry brandy. I spent many a lovely afternoon at this place and really enjoyed looking over the Bay of Naples at the peaceful surroundings.

About the third week of July we were moved again, only this time to an area just north of Naples. This was a most desolate area and though it wasn't far from Naples, it didn't have the serenity of the Sorrento area. We had one more exercise to perform, a final practice before we went off to our fourth amphibious invasion. On our last night of the practice invasion we came off our LST in the

Salerno area and as we touched the shore, someone yelled to me, "Look who's in charge on this beach!" It was our former commander in training camp at Camp Croft in South Carolina. I don't think he had ever seen combat, let alone made an amphibious invasion. It was just before daybreak and as we passed this captain, the few who remembered him shouted out profanities describing his character. He had been a bastard in training camp, and what made it even more fulfilling was that the battalion commander was walking alongside us as we had gotten off the LST, and I could see him smile in the dark as the description of this captain was shouted out along the beach. That evening we went back on our LSTs to our original point of departure.

Three days before the invasion we were loaded on our ships and sailed out of Italy to a destination that even the Germans were informed that we were headed for, but they didn't believe was true. This was the fifth ship I had been on since I left the States.

On August 14 we pulled into an area south of Corsica and during the day a few of us dove off the ship and went swimming in the warm waters of the Mediterranean Sea. After being fed C rations, the conversation had gotten around to how well our troops were doing in France; there wasn't a word spoken about the approaching invasion. We were the reserve regiment for the division and weren't supposed to land until H+4 which was around noon on August 15.

The hot sun and swim had taken their toll and many of us had fallen asleep when our ship moved out of the Corsica area to join the rest of the fleet. I awoke the next morning as our ship was almost coming to a halt. The high mountains and hills in the background looked similar to Salerno. "Not again," some of the men cried out as they saw the scenery, but our ship just kept on going slowly. Off to our right were two battleships firing their 15- and 16-inch guns in the direction of the 36th Division sector. They must have hit a storm; the guns of the battleship seemed to lift them right out of the water. The small ships that had carried in the advance troops were coming back and the companies on these ships were sunning themselves. Our sector was relatively quiet and smiles broke out on the faces of the men, where only a moment before there had been blank expressions.

The ship stopped about 5 yards from the shore and we walked off in single file and into about three feet of water. This was the first time in four landings that I had to walk in water, even though there wasn't much enemy action except for the whistle of a few bullets. No one with any experience liked to stay on the beach because one became a sitting duck to enemy fire.

Upon reaching solid ground, everyone moved forward. There was no hesitation and the next thing we knew, we were moving through St. Maxims, a resort town on the Riviera, and as we passed a walled house, I looked in through the gate. There sitting around a table with maps was the division general and his staff.

Troops were moving north automatically as long as there was no strong enemy action. As we moved forward through the area people came out to cheer us on. This was something new, and bolstered our spirits.

On the second day while walking down a road, the column was halted and we lay alongside the road. We were soon to see the reason why. Tanks of a Free French division were given preference to use the road first. They had just landed and were off to engage the enemy in another sector. While waiting for the tanks to go by, other traffic was held up on the road. Two girls on bicycles passed us and had to stop about 25 yards from us. They probably lived nearby, but while waiting one of the girl's dresses got caught on the seat of the bike, thus exposing her posterior which was completely unclothed. One of the men pointed it out to those in back and thus it soon became a focal point for everyone's eyes who could see for a hundred yards. A smile covered the GIs' faces but everyone was silent; everyone was tired.

That evening, we reached high ground and could see the shoreline and the ships unloading at a feverish pace, and then the antiaircraft guns would open up as the enemy planes flew in trying to bomb the ships in the harbor. One of the communication jeeps pulled up to where we were standing and brought in a short-wave broadcast from the BBC. The news sounded good; it was about our invasion. We found out how well we were doing and how far we had advanced into France.

The next day we advanced into a small town where we were held up for the day, and as I was standing there two soldiers came over with a girl and asked if anyone could speak French. In my best high school French I tried to interpret for them. They wanted to know where she lived, She told me to go with her, so two other soldiers I was with, Fiakovich and Kruzewski almost killed me when I told the two soldiers who had brought her to follow her and she would take them with her. My explanation to Fiakovich was that they saw her first. They never got over the incident and told almost everybody in the company.

Then the area seemed to open up. We were put on trucks and we rushed over the mountains for Grenoble. We pulled up the next morning on top of a mountain pass where members of the Free French were doing battle with some Germans and Fascist French civilians. As I walked among those captured enemy, one officer of the Free French was holding a revolver to the head of a French civilian. I thought, this guy's dead, and then he started spouting out enemy positions in French. Whether he was shot, I didn't know, but we went into the trucks and back on the treacherous mountain passes. This was the same route Napoleon had taken when he re-entered France after his escape. These mountains were more dangerous than the enemy. The Free French were a big help; they seemed to clear many of the roads of enemy troops.

We came into Grenoble, a town celebrating her freedom. This was a central position of the Free French and the townspeople let us know how much they appreciated our effort. Guns were going off all night in the center of town, but we later learned it was the Free French firing squads executing the French Fascist police and collaborators. The next morning we awoke to more gunfire but it was still coming from the area of the city hall. Then we saw what happened to French women who had been friendly with the Germans. Their hair was shaved off and then they were paraded through town to the taunts and jeers of the citizenry.

Our company had set up battalion headquarters in an old school, and while we were there, some Free French men came running and in an excited tone told us that there were some German troops up in the hills overlooking the town and we had better get some troops over there very soon before they attacked. Everyone seemed so calm that the French got more aggravated because they thought there ought to be an immediate attack. The battalion staff knew the Germans were trying to surrender, but didn't want to surrender to the Free French, only to the Americans. They feared the Free French and not without reason. The Germans did surrender early that evening to a lieutenant from our battalion and he laid them down at our aid station. Two Free French men came over to where the German wounded were laying and pulled out revolvers and aimed them at the heads of the prisoners laying on the ground. I grabbed one by the arms before he could fire and told him we didn't shoot wounded prisoners, but their hate was so great, that they spat right in the faces of the wounded prisoners. We allowed that. Of course if I had known about the concentration camps at that time, I doubt I would have stood in the way.

The next day walking in town and enjoying the fruits of our rioting, I bumped into Neil Shea. He was wearing cleaned and pressed clothes. A crease in his pants gave him the appearance of a rear echelon soldier. After the usual greetings, I asked him how come his clothes looked so good. He told me he had his own laundress; he was staying in an apartment down the road with all the services of a hotel and that went for maid service. He sure was enjoying himself.

After leaving Grenoble we turned east toward the French Alps and Switzerland. Some of the fellows thought it would be a good idea to cross the mountains and escape to Switzerland for the rest of the war. Everyone thinks of ways to get out of the war but some never attempt their plans. We continued going north and after a few days, we would soon be brought to a slow advance, so this last town where we had set up our positions in an open field without digging in as we had become somewhat lazy in the face of the slackening enemy fire. While sitting around, relaxing, someone called out my name. It was Joe Penn. "How would you like to meet a couple of Jewish girls?" I thought he was nuts. "Come with me. See that hotel that's next to the battalion CP? We're going to have supper there." I thought he was nuts, but I went along with him. It was just turning dark so we were able to sneak into the hotel without anyone seeing us. Inside there were a few candles burning as the electricity had been cut off. A woman came up to us and invited us into the dining room. She was the owner, and by the flicker of the candles, I could see two young women standing inside the dining room. They waved at us and we walked over to a table near where they were standing and the owner of the hotel told us to sit down and brought over a bottle of wine and said she would bring the food out shortly. Joe Penn introduced me to the girls, and they told us that they were staying at the hotel. Their husbands were fighting for the Free French and they were happy to meet two Jewish soldiers. Before the owner could come back with the dinner, we heard voices in the entrance of the hotel. Joe said, "Shit, it's the battalion commander and his staff. They were sleeping at the hotel and were headed for the dining room. If we had gotten caught, all hell would have broken loose; maybe not, but I thought so. I immediately blew out the candles. The owner was carrying a candle which I also blew out. The girls took us by the hand and led us out into the foyer past the battalion officers who couldn't see anything, but kept questioning what happened to the lights. We followed the girls up the stairs to their room, and they locked the door. They spoke in whispers in answer to our questions as to how they had ended up in this town and this hotel. The battalion officers knew about the girls staying at the hotel because there was soon a knock at the door, and in pretty good French a voice on the other side asked the girls if they would like to have company, maybe with a bottle of wine. While one listened the other interpreted the conversation for us. They spoke pretty good Yiddish, so we were able to hold a half way decent conversation with them. For about 45 minutes the officer on the other side of the door, who didn't know we were in the room kept whispering sweet nothings in French to the women, trying to entice them out. Finally getting tired of being unsuccessful the officers retreated back to the dining room. Joe said, "Do you know who that was whispering sweet nothings? It was the chaplain." I almost died laughing. Even men of the cloth can be swayed by a woman's skirts. But Joe and I were no luckier than the chaplain. The girls were faithful to their husbands, but it was nice meeting a couple of Jewish women on a battlefield and for a few hours listening to their ordeal under the Nazis and admiring their zeal in standing up to those almost insurmountable problems.

I got back to my former position just before daylight, and I hadn't been asleep an hour, before I heard loud noises all around me. Looking up I saw these soldiers with shovels digging foxholes.

"What are you doing?" I asked.

One soldier answered, "We were told to dig in."

As this was the front line, I tried to calm them. I answered, "We'll probably be moving on shortly and this will be a rear echelon position! You're wasting your time digging in. What outfit are you with?"

"We're division S-4," they answered.

I couldn't believe these guys. They were psycho before they heard a shot. We just laughed and waited for orders to move on while they dug foxholes.

That day about early afternoon we halted to cross a river and while we were waiting, the 1st Battalion of our regiment started going through our lines. They were taking over the point, so I looked for Neil Shea's company and sure enough they came through and Neil was driving his jeep. The line stopped and Neil yelled out, "I got something for you." It was an officer shirt—one of those soft non-wool types. Then he gave me some cigars and cigarettes and after a conversation of about fifteen minutes, he moved on. This would be the last time I would see him until I came home from the war.

We crossed the river about two hours after Neil's battalion went through and made a camp on the other side. As we were the reserve battalion, we started to take it easy, but the next day a call came down for some ammunition to be brought up to the front and as one of our trucks was loaded they sent Dave Lyons and his truck out. He asked me if I wanted to go for the ride. I was perfectly comfortable where I was, but Lieutenant Ostroff was asked by the communication lieutenant if he would take his place as he wasn't feeling well. He was supposed to head the convoy.

Relaxing as soldiers can easily do while waiting to move out, a jeep drove up to our company and a soldier came out with the bad news that the convoy had been ambushed by German tanks. Dave Lyons had been killed and Lieutenant Ostroff had been badly wounded. How lucky I was; it only went to prove that you didn't volunteer for anything in the army, especially if you didn't have to. I didn't know at the time, but that was the same area where Neil Shea was captured.

Moving out the next day we were heading in the direction of the Belfort Gap. This was the last place of escape for the Germans in southern France. The resistance had stiffened and the Germans were able to keep the area open. Now we were coming to the wooded mountains and the forward momentum of our drive had slowed. There was a shortage of men in the rifle companies and as we entered the Voagex mountains the resistance stiffened and I lost a good friend there—Harry Griffith, a sergeant in the antitank platoon. Also just before we reached the Voagex the regiment was halted for a day and as Neil Shea's battalion was close by I went over to see how he was. I saw a few of the men who knew Neil and me. They told me Neil was missing in action and that they thought he had been captured. It was a great shock to me, even though I had many people whom I had been friendly with missing or killed. This hit me very hard and for a few minutes I tried to regain my composure. Here he had such a good time in Grenoble and now he was missing! I hoped he was only a prisoner of war.

The area the battalion had to cover in the dark forest was about the size for a regiment to cover, and the rifle companies were under strength. Gaps existed between companies and if the enemy wished they could get between the gaps and outflank the battalion. Where there had been close to two hundred men in the rifle companies, some had only about one hundred men. Therefore, patrols were formed from Battalion Headquarters Company, and I was put in charge of one patrol. We dug in behind the rifle companies and every evening at dusk we would start our patrol. We contacted the CP of each line company to make sure everything was under control and tried to stop enemy patrols that we could contact. The darkness of the woods was a hard handicap to overcome, so we used white tape that each man held onto for part of the patrol. Many times we almost got shot by our own men, who nervously waited in foxholes while listening to footsteps as we approached. Then we were called on to do some daylight patrols as the enemy was active during the day behind our lines. I had to pass M Company every day and waved hello to Dave Cavanaugh, who was a machine gun sergeant. He was seated behind his section and always greeted me with a smile.

One day I heard artillery guns going off close by. Checking up I found the firing was coming from an all-Black unit. That was a cannon company; it had 90-mm guns on vehicles that looked like tanks but were open at the top and sometimes called tank destroyers. Those Black soldiers gave us a big wave as we passed on our patrol. Personally I thought their unit was too close to the front. They were even in front of the heavy weapons company mortars. These patrols were carried on for a number of days. One day I got a call to come down to the battalion CP where Captain Papianou told me I was to head up a detail to try to get supplies to K Company which was up on a hill where the fire was so great that it was difficult to get supplies to them and they were running short. He informed me that I was doing so well with these patrols that I was to lead this resupply detail and that I would have over a hundred men to lay the stuff to K Company.

I started up the road alone and though there was artillery fire breaking alongside the road, I kept going in the slight drizzle as dusk was approaching. I must have made an impression on the waiting soldiers as they saw me come up the road under fire with my carbine turned upside down and a cigarette hanging from my mouth. The soldiers consisted of sergeants and even a couple of 2nd lieutenants from rear echelons. When I got to a protected alcove, I signaled the men to gather around and explained to them that if everyone did his job with a little luck, we should accomplish our mission in a short time. Everyone had to take hold of rations, ammunition, or water cans. I wasn't going to stand over them and watch because I was going to lead the detail, and in a low tone I told them no smoking or talking until we had gotten back to our starting point. I gathered some of the men who had been on patrol with me—Pernick, Phillips, Powell, Frakowich; Knmzewson, and Long, and told them to mix up with the other men to make sure that they all did their part. Calling the runner from K Company, I told him to lead the way and he didn't have to carry anything. Grabbing a water can with Frabovich, we started up the hill. It was only a small tortuous path. It was dark so snipers were eliminated for the moment, but mortar shells could come thundering. These silent mortars could be on us before we knew what happened. Luck held out for the first load and as the last of detail came down the hill we started up with the second load. The men were businesslike and no one shirked. It was a two-hour job, and the enemy didn't even open up with their firepower.

I waited at the bottom of the hill to tell the men to go back to their units as there was no sense for them to wait around at this point. Just then Fiakovich and Kruzewski came up to me and pointed out the soldiers who hid and didn't carry anything up to K Company. They demanded that I turn them in for desertion in the face of the enemy. One of these men had made a lot of Anti-Semitic remarks to me on Anzio but later apologized. What a way to get even, I thought. So asking why they hadn't made the trip, the answer was that they were scared. My answer was "I'm just as scared as you, but I'm not a yellow bastard." I didn't take the advice of two of my men and didn't turn them in, so we went back to our unit.

No medals were handed out for this feat or for the over two weeks that I had patrolled the Vosyes mountains, but the captain gave a Silver Star to a jeep driver, who had saved a jeep in the woods from the Germans.

Our last destination before being relieved was a town by the name of Baccarat, where world famous crystal is made. So around November 5 the regiment was relieved and we went back to a rest area to enjoy a well-earned break from the front lines.

The town of Contreville was our rest area. It was a resort town with a number of hotels. This was an unusual break for the soldiers—our own hotel room, a bed to sleep on, no enemy fire to worry about, and hot food everyday. But I had a job to do. First Sergeant Frisbee had appointed me P.R. officer and noncom officer for the company, back at Anzio. Therefore, when we were in a rest area I put up a bulletin board and put up whatever newspaper articles might be of interest to the men especially articles on how the war was going on both the Russian front and on our own. Frisbee also had acquired a nice room at the hotel where he hosted poker games for the other 1st sergeants of the battalion So with five first sergeants I would sit down and indulge in a friendly poker game. I knew a few of them from the States, but got on a friendly basis with all. Frisbee managed to get Planters peanuts and some whiskey for these games; he sure was a good host. One night one of the first sergeants asked him about the bulletin that had come down from Eisenhower's headquarters. Was it true that men with over two hundred days in combat were to be relieved? I looked up in astonishment from my cards. Did I hear right? Frisbee started to stutter and then came right out and said it was true. Then he got up and walked over to a desk and passed out a few of the bulletins. Sure enough, it said after two hundred days in combat, infantrymen had lost their zeal for fighting and would be better off sent back to a rear echelon unit, and the British found their infantrymen had lost their value after 180 days in combat. Once the game was over I took one of the bulletins with me and showed it to some of the men who had that amount of time in combat. It seemed four of us had made up our minds to take advantage of this order in the next few days. Some of the men got their applications in and were preparing to leave the battalion. As for me, I told Frisbee I was going to leave. He told me to wait as he had a proposition for me. Then he told me I could be his assistant, sort of a company clerk. If something happened to him I could fill in for him. He had cleared it with the captain. I asked him why he hadn't tried to get that job for me before the pressure was on? I told him I would let him know and I waited until orders came to pull out of our hotel and back to the front. Then I joined him in his jeep. Did I make a mistake? I could have sweated out the war in some rear echelon outfit, but could I ever get adjusted to shaving every day, wearing a tie, God forbid, and even shining my shoes? Besides most of the fellows were known to me and what friends I had were with the unit, and would I be able to go back to a rear echelon unit with officers as stupid as the men they commanded? Now I wouldn't have to be exposed as in the past; so I thought.

For a week as we moved from town to town, I learned the duties of a 1st sergeant. It wasn't such a bad life. After two weeks, we had picked a pretty good house in Alsace to make battalion headquarters. Exhaustion after a long day in the field, lead to falling asleep before Frisbee. Waking up the next morning, expecting to be greeted by Sergeant Frisbee, I found myself in an empty room. What had happened to Frisbee? He usually was around when I awakened.

Some of the men from different platoons came in with their daily report. They said, "You are now the 1st sergeant."

"What are you, nuts?" I replied.

Then they told me that Frisbee had gone home on a thirty-day furlough. The son of a bitch; he hadn't said a word. Now I was a PFC acting 1st sergeant.

Now that I was operating on my own, I decided to travel with the different platoons. First, I stayed with Delano's intelligence section; they always had to set up an OP so they would usually be out a little more forward than the rest of the company, so I was still in the middle of the action.

The regiment kept moving forward until we ended up in Nuderbrown; it was some sort of resort town in northeastern Alsace not far from the German border. We found a house to stay in and a nice bed for me, as the people who lived there had moved to the cellar where they thought it was safer. They thought we were crazy to stay on the first floor. We gave them cigarettes and coffee. They said they were going to move to North Africa after the war; they were tired of war every twenty-five years. I had to bring the daily report in to battalion headquarters every day and the shelling was exceptionally heavy. The battalion moved over the hill and into German territory.

Chapter Fourteen

Germany

The story continues...now being told by Sid's lifelong friend, former Sergeant Alfred Hook.

On December 15, 1944 the 45th Division crossed the German border into the outer fringes of the Siegfried line. The fighting was very intense for now the war was being fought on German soil. The Germans fought like madmen for Hitler had promised that no foreign troop would ever set foot on German soil.

Our platoon was scattered. My job was to use mule trains, to bring food, water, and ammunition to the line companies and return with the wounded and dead. I would load the mules in the early morning while it was still dark and head up the mountains.

We had quartermaster mule skinners with us, but at the burst of the first shell, the skinners disappeared. We were lucky if they were found the next day.

The mountain was climbed using log shoots. We hung onto the mule's tails as we moved up. This process took all day as we carried supplies up and the wounded and dead down on the return trip.

About this time the Battle of the Bulge had started in the North. Two divisions and the Armored Division from the 7th Army were sent north to General Patton's 3rd Army. Their purpose was to break through the German line and rescue the 101st Airborne, who were trapped at Bastogne. This left the 7th Army short of two infantry and one armored division. The rest of the 7th Army had to take up this space making the lines very, very thin.

At this time rumors were running wild, and GIs lived on rumors. Then, my squad returned to the French Maginot Line to prepare to spend the winter there. We had our Christmas turkey dinner there, marking my third Christmas in the service, and the second Christmas spent in battle.

When the German drive was stopped in the north, German General VonRundstadt moved all of the remaining German armor south to hit the 7th Army at the Saverne Gap and the plains of Haguenau, knowing that of or our armor was in the north. Their attack on us was so sudden, and we had to move so fast in order to keep from getting cut off, that as we moved out of one end of the town, they moved in. There was no time to create road blocks, or mine the roads. In fact, that one night we lost the territory it took our 45th and 179th one month to take.

We eventually set up a command post at Wingen, with the line companies racing up the road to relieve a company that was trapped. My squad's job was to patrol from the company CP in Wingen to I Company. We were to keep the road clear from the company CP to the line companies. This was stupid because if the Germans were trying to get behind us, all they had to do was to lay low and wait until we passed. Then they could go their way as it took about an hour to make the round trip.

On January 4, 1945, we were overrun from the rear by SS troops who came from Norway. These were Hitler's elite killer-troops. I remember that day very well. We had positioned ourselves in two houses, one on each side of the road. Each house had a clear view of the town from its windows. We could see troops moving across town and half-tracks traveling up the streets and along the railroad tracks. They were our half-tracks, but manned by the Germans. We did not know this.

The first shot from the half-track hit the house across the street and the men came running out. No one was hurt. A second shot fell short of a tank just down the street from us. As we ran toward our tank, we hollered to the lieutenant there, "Aren't those tracks ours?" and then he replied, "Yes, but with SS troops in them." That was when we learned we had the Germans in front and in back of us. That's a God-awful feeling because there was no place to go!

Our tank moved slowly down the street to a corner where they could watch the half-track come up the street, make a turn and face the tank. As the Germans began to lower the gun in the half-track, the tank fired one round and the track went up in smoke. That was the first time we had seen a tank battle up close. In addition to this, the Germans had captured the 1st Battalion Headquarters company

By January 7, the Germans in Wingen knew that no help was coming and they tried to escape by night, but not very many of them made it. A few days later we moved out and took Althorn and the German drive was over for now.

Both sides took one hell of a beating; they much more than us. I don't want you to think we never lost men, for we did—a lot of them. The only time it really bothered us was when it was someone we knew. I do not know where Sid was during these days, as there were many times when we did not see the other two squads for days.

About this time we got a break. Lieutenant K, our platoon leader knew someone in the Quartermaster Corps. He went to see his friend and returned with a 6 x 6 truck loaded with the kind of food you get in stores. For a few days we ate like kings! (There is always some GI who knows how to get things, even if they had to be stolen!)

Soon our few days of rest came to an end and the war moved us on. It was February 17 when the 179th went into bivouac area around Rambervillers. It was there, on February 19 that I was relieved of duty and sent to London for ten days R & R. Having no money at the time, Andy Kovaly played poker all night and gave me his winnings to have while in London and Paris. (Thirty-eight years later I saw Andy again and, after a few minutes, he asked me when I was going to pay back the money he gave me to go to London!)

When I returned to the company, they were on the move to the Rhine River, and the men were all dog tired. It seemed to be a race to see who could take the most territory and the most prisoners yet still keep going twenty-four hours at a time. We would get a few hours rest and then be on the move again.

Orders called for the 179th and the 180th to lead the attack across the Rhine River. On the night of March 23 the regiment crossed the Rhine under heavy fire, and by daylight both regiments were across, but not without casualties.

We moved 40 miles in thirty hours, taking town after town. Military equipment was strewn all over the place. Then we came to the city of Aschoffenburg, the key to the German defenses in that area. In fact, we later learned the German commander of the area gave orders for everyone, civilians and all, to fight to the death.

But before I get to that part, let me tell of a funny thing that happened. Word had gotten to the battalion commander, Lt. Colonel Riggs, that one of the other battalion commanders had found a warehouse full of whiskey. Colonel Riggs loved his liquor so word came down to send a truck over to the warehouse. We had a 5-ton German truck, so a squad of men and Lieutenant Cox plus Sid, who had his own car by now, decided to go. Sid said he knew the way, so off they went at dusk, Sid and Lieutenant Cox, with the truck following.

Now, at night everything looks different. So they took the wrong road and found themselves between the lines—in no man's land! A bridge had been blown up, so into the creek went the car. The truck, trying to avoid the car, joined it, making so much noise both sides began to drop mortars in the area.

The men made their way down stream until an American patrol met them and they were taken to an aid station. The company commander wanted to know what in the hell they were doing there, as that was where the machine gun nest was. All the boys could say was that they got lost and took the wrong road. Most of the men were cut up and later were given Purple Hearts—all but the leader of the gang, Sid. The only thing he got was blame for losing the truck. And the CO got no whiskey!

As the battle for Aschoffenburg went on, we out-flanked the city and took the hills. When the battle was over, we found the bodies of hundreds of young boys, ten to fifteen years old, who had been part of the line. As hard as we were to death and wounds which we lived with every day, it made us sick to see these boys. I saw tears in the men's eyes as they realized who we had been fighting. Aschoffenburg, deep in Germany, fell 100 percent destroyed. It was a city of 90,000 men, women, and children.

Leaving Aschoffenburg behind, we rolled on mile after mile, town after town, to do battle after battle. About April 4 or 5 we were again hit by our old enemies, the SS—the same ones who hit us in Wingen in January. We kept moving one battalion through another. When one got tired, the other moved through the lines. It was like playing leap frog.

It was at this time, and funny to see, but there were groups of German soldiers waiting by the roads, ready to surrender. But we didn't have the time for them, so we took their weapons and sent them to the rear. Then someone down the road would take them to the stockade for the duration and to the army to take care of them, as the war was over for them.

On the morning of April 8, we were on the move again. We took eight towns and had the honor of capturing Major General Franz, his artillery company and his chief of staff. We knew him well, for he was the commander of the SS troops who fought us in Wingen. Now the general and his 256 command were no more!

That night we moved on with our artillery, cleaning out pockets of enemies for us when they could.

On April 9, the 179th was ordered to clear the area of any Germans, and we were to be put in reserve. Then on April 11 orders came to move at once. No chance to get any rest now, for we were on our way to take Banberg, as the Germans were not ready to lay down their arms. They fought savagely for every town. But in every town we took, the people were glad that there would be no more bombing. They took orders from us, but did not like it.

It was about this time that we learned that President Roosevelt had died. To this day I don't know how I felt because the night we crossed the Rhine River I got word from home that my younger brother had been killed so one more death didn't mean so much to me. It took me years to get over my brother's death. I think if I could have seen him, I would have gotten over it sooner.

It was all we could do to stay alive. Don't think that as we rolled through the countryside that we didn't have casualties, for we had many. About this time we were hit by another of the enemy's weapons—the first of the German jets—the Air Corps didn't know what hit them.

The smell of death and the acid smell of gun powder were everywhere. We couldn't escape it. There were times we had to wait until the engineers rebuilt bridges over the rivers so we could get trucks and tanks across and the artillery could catch up with us. The infantry can't get too far ahead without food and ammunition.

From Banberg, the road for the 179th was to Nürnburg, the birthplace of Nazism. On April 14, we were moving as fast as we could go. Division ordered every unit to commit reserves the moment any assault unit was held up. There was to be no stopping; no matter how tired the men were. But on April 20, the fighting was over. Nürnburg was in Allied hands. The 157th was the first unit of the 45th to enter the city. We had fought in three countries, but nowhere had we seen such destruction. Nürnburg was in ruins. It was possible to stand in the center of the city and look for miles as our view was unobstructed.

On April 22, the 179th Regiment moved south again toward Munich, 148 kilometers away. In one day we took 30 kilometers of territory. On the morning of April 26, exactly one month after crossing the Rhine River, 400 miles away, the 179th stood on the banks of the Danube, the last major river to cross. This river was green, not blue. It was very deep and very swift.

That afternoon, after the line companies had crossed, I went with the squad and a boatload of ammunition. By now the battalion was in the town of Neuburg and needed ammunition. Having no truck and it being too far to carry, we rounded up all the German prisoners we could get from the MPs and made them carry ammunition all night. We even had one woman prisoner.

The next morning Captain P and I started to look for a truck to move the ammunition so we could keep up with the lines. We found a car, but the German woman didn't want to give it to us. Someone who spoke English told us the woman wanted a receipt for it, so captain P gave her a note saying, "I took your car. Tough shit." I wonder if she ever got it back. Probably not.

By early afternoon the TDs came over the river. We hopped on the tank and began pulling roadblocks so trucks could get through. We did that nearly all night. Also at Neuburg, we found an underground airplane factory under a pine forest. We had never seen anything like it before, or after.

On April 29, General Fredricks ordered the whole division into the attack, as we were only 20 miles from Munich, and the race was on for the final plans for the capture of Munich. On April 30 the final push began. The 2nd Battalion moved out leading the attack and was the first to enter the city. By the end of April 30, the city had fallen and the 157th had continued on to Dachau, the concentration camp.

May 3 was the day the division was told that the war was over for us, and we were never to fight again. The 179th was given the job of guarding the municipal buildings of the city. My squad was quartered in the Museum of Natural History of Bavaria.

In the latter part of May or early June, we were moved to the town. of Mossburg. There was a large American prisoner of war camp there. The prisoners had all been released by the time we got there. We reverted back to garrison days while there, with all of us having various duties. Sid went back to the CP. I had the job of doing night patrol of the town—one jeep, one machine gun, two men, and a German cop.

In the latter part of June, the high-point men were getting ready to come home when word got out that the 45th was to be shipped home, and then on to the Pacific to fight the Japs. As if we hadn't done our part!

During the first part of July we were shipped out for Innsbruck, Austria, the start of the Brenner Pass in the Alps. There, we were taken out of the 45th and put into the 103rd to come home. On July 4, we had gone all the way went up on the mountain to a Red Cross lodge and drank the last of the whiskey we got when Munich fell.

We didn't stay in Innsbruck too long, but went by truck to Landsburg, Germany. Again we had various jobs to do. Sid went back to the CP as a clerk. We both lived in the same house. I had the job of transporting wounded German soldiers from the hospital in Lansburg to the hospital in Munich, so they could be discharged.

By late August or early September we were shipped by boxcar to Camp Lucky Strike in LeHavre, France. We could not get out of this camp, as we were given medical exams every day. No one could leave this camp unless he was medically fit. Here we remained for seven days. Finally the day arrived when we were moved by truck to the port of LeHavre. The ship was nice compared to the one we left the states on, the old *Florence Nightingale*. It had been twenty-seven months since we left Newport News, Virginia.

One thing I will never forget as long as I live. As we stood on the tail of the ship and the coastline of France faded in the sunset Sid said to those who were present, "By rights, we have no business going home. We all should have been dead after what we have been through."

We finally landed in New York where we stayed at Camp Shanks for a few days. It was there that we said out good-byes, amid many tears, to the comrades we served with, and some never to see again.

Sid, Veto Fruci, Wally Colito, Louis Filosi, and I went to Fort Devens, the starting place for most of us years ago. At Devens we went on furlough together—the first furlough for me in three years. We took the train to Boston, went to a bar, had a drink together, and then went our separate ways for a week. Most of us had some very hard things to face when we first saw our families. Things had changed a lot in the three years we had been gone.

Seven days later we were once again back in Fort Devens, waiting to be separated from the army, and to return to civilization, as we called it. On the third of October, we were discharged.

We have seen one another many times over the years. I do not think there is a stronger bond between any men than there is between the ones we lived with, ate with, fought with, and served with all those years.

Dick Long passed away January 1989. and Sid in May 1989. I am the last of the men who stood on that ship as it sailed into the sunset so many years ago. Sid, wherever you are, I'm thinking of you.

As I told Sid's wife Jeannette when she asked me to help finish this story, "I can't tell it in Sid's words, but I'll try to finish it the way he would have wanted it."

Al Hook

June 1990